Set, Simmer, & Savor It!

Set, Simmer, & Savor It!

**More Than 75 Easy Recipes
for the Slow Cooker**

Compiled by Anne Sheasby

AN IMPRINT OF RUNNING PRESS
PHILADELPHIA • LONDON

2003 Salamander Books Ltd
Published by Salamander Books Ltd.
The Chrysalis Building, Bramley Road
London W10 6SP, United Kingdom

© Salamander Books Ltd., 2003

An imprint of **Chrysalis** Books Group plc

This edition published in the United States by Courage Books, an imprint of
Running Press Book Publishers
125 South Twenty-second Street
Philadelphia, PA 19103-4399

3 5 7 9 8 6 4 2

Library of Congress Cataloguing-in-Publication Number 2002116201
ISBN 0-7624-1535-5

Notice: The information contained in this book is true and complete to the best of our knowledge. All
recommendations are made without any guarantee on the part of the author or publisher. The author and
publisher disclaim all liability in connection with the use of this information.

Credits

Project Manager: Anne McDowall
Commissioning Editor: Stella Caldwell
Designers: twelveotwo
Production: Ian Hughes
Color reproduction: Anorax Imaging Ltd.
Printed in China

The recipes in this book have appeared in previous Salamander titles by other authors and have been
compiled by Anne Sheasby and edited by Anne McDowall for this edition.

Notes

All spoon measurements are level: 1 teaspoon = 5ml spoon; 1 tablespoon = 15ml spoon

This book may be ordered by mail from the publisher. But try your bookstore first!

Visit us on the web!
www.runningpress.com

Contents

Introduction

Although they have been around for years, slow cookers are only now making a well-deserved comeback. Slow cooking is the perfect way to prepare a wide variety of delicious food, from soups and stews to fondues and fruit compotes, and it's hard to beat the aroma of a delicious casserole, perfectly cooked and ready to eat, when you arrive home at the end of a tiring day!

Slow cookers are simple and economical to use and require little or no attention once the ingredients for your recipe have been prepared ready for cooking. Foods are usually cooked for long periods of time, so ingredients such as meat – even the cheapest, toughest cuts – and vegetables become deliciously tender. Slow cooking also retains all the goodness and develops the flavor of foods. There is little evaporation, so food doesn't dry out.

Choosing a slow cooker

A good selection of slow cookers is now widely available, many at a modest price, in a range of shapes and colors and varying in capacity from approximately 2¹/₂ pints to 5 or 6 quarts. All slow cookers operate at a low wattage and consume a similar amount of electricity and the efficient insulation built into the appliance ensures that only the food inside the slow cooker heats up and not the whole kitchen.

There are two main types of slow cooker. The most common ones have a removable inner earthenware or ceramic cooking pot. The outer casing of these models is usually made of metal or heat-resistant plastic and is fitted with an inner metal casing. The removable cooking pot sits in the inner casing and the heating elements are situated between the inner and outer casings. Lids are made of heat-resistant glass or ceramic.

Other less common types comprise an earthenware or ceramic pot that is permanently fixed into an outer casing. The heating elements are housed between the outer casing and the cooking pot.

Using a slow cooker

Always read through the manufacturer's instructions before using your slow cooker for the first time. Models vary slightly and even on the same setting, some will cook faster or slower than others. Use your slow cooker several times before trying the recipes in this book; the timings given are intended to be an accurate guide, but you may find that your model cooks more quickly or more slowly and that you need to adjust the cooking times accordingly.

Most slow cookers have three basic settings – OFF, LOW and HIGH; others also include an AUTO setting. Most models have a power indicator light. On the LOW setting, the slow cooker will cook foods very gently with hardly any simmering. On the HIGH setting, the cooker may actually boil some foods and liquids. With the AUTO setting, cooking starts at a high temperature, then automatically switches to a LOW cook and the temperature is thermostatically controlled. Most of the recipes in this book use the HIGH or LOW settings.

The slow cooker may need to be preheated on HIGH about 20 minutes (refer to the manufacturer's instructions for your specific model). You can often use this time to prepare the ingredients for cooking. To preheat your slow cooker (if applicable), simply place the empty cooking pot in the slow cooker base, place the lid in position, plug in, and switch on with the control set on HIGH. Once the cooker is preheated, add the prepared ingredients to the cooking pot, replace the lid, and continue cooking as directed in the recipe.

Adapting your own recipes

Once you are used to using your slow cooker, you will easily be able to adapt your own recipes to cook in the slow cooker. Simply refer to similar recipes in this book or in the manufacturer's instruction book and change cooking times accordingly.

It is also worth remembering, however, that because there is less evaporation in a slow cooker, you will almost always need to reduce the quantity of liquid used. In a slow cooker, steam condenses on the lid and returns to the pot and, in doing so, forms a seal around the lid that retains heat and flavor.) As a guide, use about half the quantity of liquid given in a conventional recipe – you can always add a little more boiling liquid at the end of the cooking time if the cooked result is too thick. If you wish to reduce the quantity of liquid at the end of the cooking time, remove the lid after cooking, turn the setting to HIGH, and reduce by simmering an additional 30 to 45 minutes.

Tips for slow cooking

◆ Unless the recipe specifies otherwise, do not lift the lid during the cooking process, as this will break the water seal around the rim and will interfere with the cooking time. (With most recipes, there is no need to turn or stir the food, as it will not stick, burn, or bubble over, and slow cooking provides a very even method of cooking.)

◆ If you do need to lift the lid while cooking, remember to increase the cooking time by about 20 to 30 minutes in order to allow the slow cooker to regain lost heat.

◆ If you need to speed up the cooking process, simply switch the control to the HIGH setting. As an approximate guide, the cooking time on HIGH is just over half of that on LOW.

◆ Dishes to be cooked in a slow cooker should always contain some liquid.

◆ When cooking joints of meat or foods that are cooked in dishes such as pudding basins, ensure that the food or dish fits comfortably in the cooking pot and that the lid fits securely before you begin to prepare the recipe.

◆ Ideally slow cookers should be filled to a maximum of $1/2$ to 1 inch from the top of the cooking pot. Make sure that the cooking pot is at least half full and no more than three-quarters full.

◆ Once cooking time is complete, you can keep food hot by switching the setting to LOW.

◆ If at the end of cooking time the food is not ready, replace the lid, switch the setting to HIGH, and continue cooking an additional 30 to 60 minutes, or until the food is thoroughly cooked.

◆ With dishes such as soups and casseroles, once the cooking time is complete, always stir the dish well before serving.

◆ Cakes cooked in a slow cooker do not brown in the way that they do when baked in a conventional oven, so they are often paler in color – though they taste just as good! Icing spread on top of a cooked cake, or sugar or nuts sprinkled over the top of it, will improve its appearance.

◆ Where a recipe for a cake or dessert calls for a cake tin, always use one with a fixed/non-removable bottom (rather than a loose-bottomed or springform one).

◆ Cold cooked food should not be reheated in the slow cooker, as it will not reach a high enough temperature to be safe.

Slow cookers with removable cooking pots are more versatile than those in which the pot is permanently fixed into an outer casing.

Preparing food for slow cooking

Trim excess fat from meat and cut meat into small, even, bite-size pieces. Cut vegetables, especially root vegetables, into small dice or thin slices. (Surprisingly, vegetables often take longer to cook than meat in a slow cooker.) Place the diced vegetables in the bottom or towards the bottom half of the cooking pot and ensure that they are covered completely with liquid.

You can speed up the cooking a little by precooking vegetables in oil or butter in a pan to soften before adding them to the slow cooker. Pre-browning or sealing meat in oil or melted butter in a pan before adding it to the slow cooker also improves the appearance, texture and flavor of the cooked food. It is often a good idea to bring the cooking liquid to a boil before adding it to the slow cooker.

If you don't have time to precook vegetables or meat, preheat the slow cooker on HIGH while preparing the ingredients. Place the chopped vegetables in the bottom of the cooking pot, add the meat or poultry, then add herbs or seasonings and pour over enough boiling stock or liquid to just cover the food. Switch the setting to LOW and cook as instructed – you will need to add about 2 to 3 hours to the minimum recommended cooking time.

Food to be slow cooked should be seasoned lightly with salt and pepper, especially salt. Add the minimum amount of salt and then check and adjust the seasoning before serving.

Always defrost frozen ingredients thoroughly before placing them in a slow cooker. Defrosted frozen vegetables are usually added towards the end of the cooking time.

Soak dried beans in plenty of cold water at least 10 hours, or overnight, then drain, place in a large pan, cover with fresh cold water, and boil 10 minutes. Drain them and use as required. Red kidney beans should be boiled rapidly 10 minutes, to kill any toxins present. Lentils do not need precooking. Use easy/quick-cooking varieties of rice and pasta.

To avoid separation or curdling, dairy products, such as cream and milk, are best added towards the end of the cooking time – or at the end of cooking, if possible. Use whole (full-fat/full-cream) milk, rather than semi-skimmed or skimmed milk.

Use dried herbs rather than fresh ones. Dried herbs tend to create a better flavor during the long, slow cooking process. (To further enhance the flavor and appearance of a dish, you can stir chopped fresh herbs into the finished dish or sprinkle them on top, if desired.)

Caring for and cleaning a slow cooker

- Refer to the manufacturer's guidelines about caring for and cleaning your slow cooker.
- Do not subject the cooking pot to sudden changes in temperature and never plunge it into cold or boiling water.
- Do not leave the pot immersed in water as this may adversely affect the porous bottom.
- Remove any stubborn stains with a soft brush or nylon cleaning pad. Do not use abrasive cleaners or scourers on the cooking pot or outer casing of your slow cooker.
- The outer casing of the slow cooker should never be immersed in water, filled with liquid or food or used for cooking without the inner cooking pot. To clean, wipe the outer casing with a cloth soaked in warm, soapy water.
- Most cooking pots and lids are not suitable for washing in a dishwasher and many cannot be placed in an oven, freezer or microwave or on a conventional stovetop – check the manufacturer's instructions for your model.
- After cooking, always use oven gloves to remove the cooking pot from the slow cooker base (and when removing the lid), as the pot (and lid) will be hot.

Soups and Appetizers

Roasted Tomato Soup with Coriander

8 RIPE PLUM TOMATOES

½ CUP OLIVE OIL

1 TABLESPOON CHOPPED
FRESH THYME

2 TEASPOONS GRATED LEMON ZEST

1 LEEK, FINELY CHOPPED

2 GARLIC CLOVES, CHOPPED

1 TABLESPOON GROUND CORIANDER

⅔ CUP WHITE WINE

4 SLICES DAY-OLD WHITE BREAD

3¾ CUPS VEGETABLE STOCK

2 TABLESPOONS CHOPPED
FRESH CILANTRO

1 TABLESPOON LEMON JUICE

◆ Preheat oven to 450°F. Quarter tomatoes and place in one layer on a large baking tray. Drizzle over ¼ cup oil and sprinkle over thyme, lemon zest, and some sea salt. Roast 30 minutes until tomatoes are charred and very mushy.

◆ Preheat the slow cooker on HIGH. Heat 2 tablespoons oil in a saucepan and sauté leek, garlic, and coriander 5 minutes. Add wine and boil 3 minutes.

◆ Remove and discard crusts from bread and crumble. Add bread, tomatoes, and stock and bring to a boil. Transfer to the cooking pot, cover, reduce temperature to LOW, and cook 4 to 6 hours.

◆ Cool slightly, purée, then return to rinsed-out cooking pot, cover, and cook on LOW 30 to 60 minutes, or until hot.

◆ Blend remaining oil, fresh cilantro, and lemon juice together and drizzle over soup. Serve with warm Italian bread, if desired.

Potato and Garlic Soup with Pesto

MAKES 4 TO 6 SERVINGS

2 HEADS GARLIC

5 CUPS VEGETABLE STOCK

1 BAY LEAF

2 PARSLEY AND 2 THYME SPRIGS

2 TABLESPOONS OLIVE OIL

1 ONION, CHOPPED

1 TEASPOON GROUND CUMIN

5 MEDIUM FLOURY POTATOES,
PEELED AND DICED

4 TO 6 TABLESPOONS PESTO,
TO SERVE

◆ Preheat slow cooker on HIGH 15 minutes. Separate garlic cloves, peel, and place in a saucepan with stock and ½ teaspoon sea salt. Tie bay leaf, parsley, and thyme in a piece of cheesecloth and add to pan. Bring to boil, transfer to cooking pot, cover, and cook on HIGH 1 to 2 hours. Discard muslin bag and make stock up to 5 cups with water.

◆ Heat oil in a large clean saucepan and sauté onion and cumin 5 minutes. Add potatoes and sauté 5 minutes. Pour in garlic broth and bring to boil. Transfer to rinsed-out cooking pot, cover, reduce to LOW, and cook 6 to 8 hours or until vegetables are cooked and tender.

◆ Cool slightly, then purée soup in a blender or food processor. Season to taste, return to the cooking pot, and cook on LOW 30 to 60 minutes.

◆ Spoon soup into bowls and stir a tablespoon of pesto into each.

Parsnip Soup with Nutmeg

MAKES 4 TO 6 SERVINGS

2 TABLESPOONS OLIVE OIL

4 MEDIUM PARSNIPS,
CUT INTO CHUNKS

1 LARGE POTATO, CUT INTO CHUNKS

1 LARGE ONION, CHOPPED

3¾ CUPS VEGETABLE STOCK

SALT AND GROUND BLACK PEPPER

2 TABLESPOONS PLAIN YOGURT

LARGE PINCH FRESHLY
GRATED NUTMEG

PLAIN YOGURT AND FRESHLY GRATED
NUTMEG, TO GARNISH

◆ Preheat the slow cooker on HIGH while preparing ingredients. Heat oil in a large saucepan, add parsnips, potato, and onion and sauté 5 minutes.

◆ Add stock and seasoning and bring to a boil. Transfer to the cooking pot, cover, reduce temperature to LOW, and cook 6 to 8 hours, or until vegetables are cooked and tender.

◆ Cool slightly, then purée soup in a blender or food processor. Return soup to the rinsed-out cooking pot and stir in yogurt and nutmeg. Cover and cook on LOW 30 to 60 minutes, or until heated through.

◆ Pour into warmed bowls, swirl in a little yogurt, sprinkle with nutmeg and serve.

Fresh Mushroom Soup

MAKES 4 SERVINGS

¹/₄ CUP DRIED PORCINI MUSHROOMS

2 TABLESPOONS BUTTER

1 ONION, FINELY CHOPPED

2 CUPS THINLY SLICED MUSHROOMS

3 CUPS VEGETABLE STOCK

SALT AND GROUND BLACK PEPPER

²/₃ CUP LIGHT CREAM

2 TABLESPOONS CHOPPED FRESH FLAT-LEAF PARSLEY

◆ Preheat the slow cooker on HIGH while preparing ingredients. Place dried mushrooms in a small bowl, pour over ¹/₂ cup boiling water, and let soak 20 minutes.

◆ Drain mushrooms, reserving soaking liquid, then snip mushrooms into small pieces using scissors. Set aside.

◆ Melt butter in a pan, add onion, and sauté 3 minutes. Add mushrooms and soaked dried mushrooms and cook gently 5 minutes, stirring occasionally. Stir in stock, reserved mushroom liquid, and seasoning, then bring to a boil.

◆ Transfer to the cooking pot, cover, reduce the temperature to LOW, and cook 5 hours.

◆ Stir in cream, cover, and cook on LOW an additional 30 to 60 minutes, or until hot.

◆ Alternatively, cool soup slightly, purée in a blender or food processor until smooth, then return to the rinsed-out cooking pot. Stir in cream, cover, and cook on LOW 30 to 60 minutes or until hot.

◆ Stir in chopped parsley and serve with warm Italian bread, if desired.

Potato, Leek and Tomato Soup

2 MEDIUM LEEKS, WHITE PART ONLY,
THINLY SLICED

2 MEDIUM POTATOES,
PEELED AND DICED

2 TABLESPOONS BUTTER

2 OR 3 MEDIUM WELL-FLAVORED
TOMATOES, CHOPPED

SALT AND GROUND BLACK PEPPER

LIGHT CREAM, TO TASTE

FINELY CHOPPED FRESH CHERVIL
OR PARSLEY, TO GARNISH

◆ Preheat the slow cooker on HIGH while preparing ingredients. Sauté leeks and potatoes in melted butter in a saucepan 5 minutes.

◆ Add tomatoes and continue to cook until they start to give up their juices, then add 3½ cups water and seasoning.

◆ Bring to a boil, then transfer to the cooking pot. Cover, reduce temperature to LOW, and cook 6 to 8 hours, or until potatoes are cooked and tender.

◆ Cool slightly, then pass soup through a vegetable mill, or purée it very briefly in a blender and press through a strainer.

◆ Return soup to the rinsed-out cooking pot, cover, and cook on LOW 30 to 60 minutes or until hot, adding a little cream to taste and adjusting consistency with extra boiling water, if necessary.

◆ Serve garnished with a fine sprinkling of chopped chervil or parsley. Serve with fresh crusty bread, if desired.

Spiced Vichyssoise

MAKES 4 SERVINGS

½ STICK BUTTER

4 LEEKS, FINELY CHOPPED

1 ONION, FINELY CHOPPED

2 OR 3 TEASPOONS MILD
CURRY PASTE

2 MEDIUM POTATOES, DICED

4 CUPS CHICKEN OR
VEGETABLE STOCK

SALT AND GROUND BLACK PEPPER

⅔ TO ¾ CUP LIGHT CREAM

FRESH CILANTRO, TO GARNISH

◆ Preheat the slow cooker on HIGH while preparing ingredients. Melt butter in a saucepan and sauté leeks and onion 5 minutes until softened. Stir in curry paste and potatoes and sauté 2 or 3 minutes, then add stock and seasoning and bring to a boil.

◆ Transfer to the cooking pot, cover, reduce temperature to LOW, and cook 6 to 8 hours, or until vegetables are completely soft.

◆ Let cool slightly, then purée briefly in a blender (potatoes quickly turn"gluey"). Adjust level of curry paste and seasoning if necessary.

◆ Stir in cream, cover, and chill. Garnish with cilantro and serve with fresh bread rolls, if desired.

Thai-Spiced Chicken Soup

2 TABLESPOONS SUNFLOWER OIL

6 SHALLOTS, FINELY CHOPPED

5 MEDIUM CARROTS,
THINLY SLICED

4 STALKS CELERY, THINLY SLICED

1 GARLIC CLOVE, CRUSHED

1 RED CHILE, SEEDED
AND FINELY CHOPPED

1-INCH PIECE FRESH GINGER,
PEELED AND FINELY CHOPPED

1 POUND SKINLESS BONELESS
CHICKEN THIGHS, DICED

1 TABLESPOON
THAI 7-SPICE SEASONING

1 CUP SLICED GREEN BEANS

3¾ CUPS CHICKEN STOCK

SALT AND GROUND BLACK PEPPER

1 CUP SPAGHETTI, BROKEN INTO
SMALL LENGTHS

2 OR 3 TABLESPOONS CHOPPED
FRESH CILANTRO

◆ Preheat the slow cooker on HIGH while preparing ingredients.

◆ Heat oil in a pan, add shallots, carrots, celery, garlic, chile, and ginger and sauté 3 minutes. Add chicken and cook until sealed all over, stirring frequently.

◆ Add Thai spice and green beans and cook 1 minute, stirring. Add stock and seasoning and bring to a boil. Transfer to the cooking pot, cover, then reduce temperature to LOW and cook 5 hours.

◆ Stir in spaghetti, cover, and cook on LOW an additional 1 to 2 hours, or until spaghetti is cooked and tender.

◆ Stir in the chopped cilantro and serve with fresh crusty bread, if desired.

Bacon and Corn Chowder

MAKES 4 TO 6 SERVINGS

2 TABLESPOONS BUTTER

8 OUNCES LEAN SMOKED BACON, DICED

1 LARGE ONION, CHOPPED

3 STALKS CELERY, FINELY CHOPPED

2 MEDIUM POTATOES, PEELED AND FINELY DICED

1 CUP SLICED BUTTON MUSHROOMS

3¾ CUPS VEGETABLE STOCK

SALT AND GROUND BLACK PEPPER

12-OUNCE CAN CORN KERNELS, DRAINED

4 TO 6 TABLESPOONS LIGHT CREAM

¼ CUP CHOPPED FRESH PARSLEY

◆ Preheat the slow cooker on HIGH while preparing ingredients. Melt butter in a pan, add bacon, and cook 3 minutes, stirring.

◆ Add onion, celery, and potatoes and sauté 5 minutes. Add mushrooms, stock, and seasoning and stir to mix. Bring to a boil.

◆ Transfer soup to the cooking pot. Cover, reduce temperature to LOW, and cook 6 hours.

◆ Stir in corn, cover, and cook on LOW an additional 1 to 2 hours. Stir in cream and chopped parsley and adjust seasoning to taste.

◆ Ladle into warmed soup bowls and serve with warm crusty bread or cornmeal bread, if desired.

Variation
Thicken soup with a little cornstarch, if desired: blend 1 to 2 tablespoons cornstarch with a little water and stir into soup. Cook on HIGH 20 to 30 minutes.

Creamy Watercress Soup

2 TABLESPOONS BUTTER

6 SHALLOTS, FINELY CHOPPED

1 LEEK, THINLY SLICED

1 LARGE OR 2 MEDIUM POTATOES, PEELED AND DICED

3 TO 4 CUPS ROUGHLY CHOPPED WATERCRESS

3½ CUPS VEGETABLE STOCK

SALT AND GROUND BLACK PEPPER

⅔ CUP LIGHT CREAM

◆ Preheat the slow cooker on HIGH while preparing ingredients.

◆ Melt butter in a pan, add shallots and leek, and sauté 5 minutes. Add potatoes and watercress and cook 3 minutes, or until watercress wilts, stirring occasionally.

◆ Add stock and seasoning, then bring to a boil. Transfer to the cooking pot, cover, reduce temperature to LOW, and cook 6 to 7 hours.

◆ Cool slightly, then purée mixture in a blender or food processor until smooth. Return soup to the rinsed-out cooking pot and stir in cream. Cover and cook on LOW 30 to 60 minutes, or until hot.

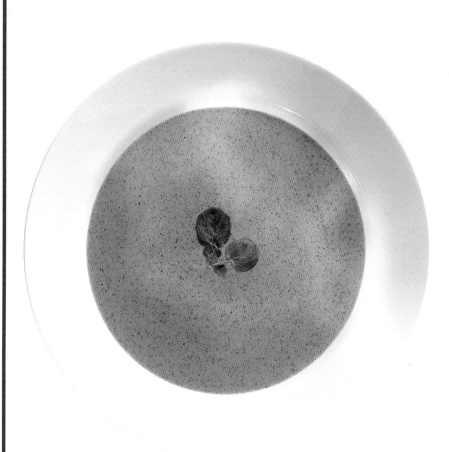

Mexican Bean Soup

MAKES 4 TO 6 SERVINGS

1¼ CUPS DRIED RED KIDNEY BEANS,
SOAKED OVERNIGHT

2 TABLESPOONS OLIVE OIL

2 RED ONIONS, FINELY CHOPPED

2 GARLIC CLOVES, CRUSHED

1 RED BELL PEPPER,
SEEDED AND DICED

1 FRESH RED CHILE, SEEDED
AND FINELY CHOPPED

2 TEASPOONS GROUND CORIANDER

1 TEASPOON GROUND CUMIN

14-OUNCE CAN CHOPPED TOMATOES

3¾ CUPS VEGETABLE STOCK

3 TEASPOONS CHILI SAUCE,
PLUS EXTRA TO TASTE

SALT AND GROUND BLACK PEPPER

2 TO 3 TABLESPOONS CHOPPED
FRESH CILANTRO

¼ CUP THICK SOURED CREAM
(OPTIONAL)

Variation
Once cooked, cool soup slightly,
purée in a blender or food processor
until smooth, then reheat on LOW 30
to 60 minutes or until hot.

◆ Preheat slow cooker on HIGH while preparing ingredients. Drain kidney beans, place in a large pan, cover with cold water, and bring to a boil. Boil rapidly 10 minutes, then rinse, drain, and set aside.

◆ Meanwhile, heat oil in a large pan, add onions, garlic, pepper, and chile and sauté 5 minutes. Add ground coriander and cumin and cook gently 1 minute, stirring.

◆ Add kidney beans, tomatoes, stock, chili sauce, and seasoning and bring to a boil. Transfer to the cooking pot, cover, reduce temperature to LOW, and cook 8 to 12 hours.

◆ Stir in chopped cilantro and extra chili sauce, if desired. Stir in soured cream, if using, and ladle into warmed soup bowls.

Plum Tomato Soup

MAKES 6 SERVINGS

8 PLUM TOMATOES

2 TABLESPOONS OLIVE OIL

1 LARGE RED ONION, THINLY SLICED

2 GARLIC CLOVES, CRUSHED

1 RED BELL PEPPER, PEELED,
SEEDED, AND THINLY SLICED

2 TABLESPOONS
SUN-DRIED TOMATO PASTE

2 TEASPOONS GRANULATED SUGAR

3¾ CUPS VEGETABLE STOCK

SALT AND GROUND BLACK PEPPER

FRESH PARMESAN SHAVINGS,
TO SERVE (OPTIONAL)

◆ Preheat the slow cooker on HIGH while preparing ingredients. Using a sharp knife, cut a small cross in the base of each tomato. Place tomatoes in a bowl, cover with boiling water, and leave 30 seconds. Using a slotted spoon, remove and plunge into cold water, then drain well. Peel off and discard skins, then chop flesh and set aside.

◆ Heat oil in a large pan, add onion, garlic, and red bell pepper and sauté 5 minutes. Stir in tomatoes, sun-dried tomato paste, sugar, stock, and seasoning, then bring to a boil.

◆ Transfer to cooking pot and cover. Switch setting to AUTO and cook 8 to 10 hours.

◆ Cool soup slightly, then purée mixture in a blender or food processor until smooth. Return soup to cooking pot, cover, and cook on LOW 30 to 60 minutes, or until hot. Sprinkle Parmesan shavings over soup to serve, if desired.

Celeriac and Dill Soup

MAKES 4 TO 6 SERVINGS

½ STICK BUTTER

1 BAY LEAF

2 TABLESPOONS CHOPPED
FRESH DILL

1 ONION, FINELY CHOPPED

1 MEDIUM CELERIAC,
WEIGHING ABOUT 1¼ POUNDS,
CUT INTO SMALL CUBES

3¾ CUPS GOOD, STRONG
VEGETABLE STOCK

SALT AND GROUND BLACK PEPPER

3 TABLESPOONS LIGHT CREAM

2 TEASPOONS LEMON JUICE

◆ Preheat the slow cooker on HIGH while preparing ingredients. Melt butter in a saucepan with bay leaf and 1 tablespoon dill. Simmer over a gentle heat 1 or 2 minutes to allow flavors to develop.

◆ Add onion and celeriac, cover, and simmer gently about 10 minutes until softened. Add stock and seasoning and bring to boil.

◆ Transfer to the cooking pot, cover, reduce temperature to LOW, and cook 6 to 8 hours, or until vegetables are tender. Remove bay leaf.

◆ Cool slightly, then purée soup in a blender or food processor until smooth. Return to the rinsed-out cooking pot, cover, and cook on LOW 30 to 60 minutes, or until hot.

◆ Stir in cream, lemon juice, and remaining dill. Check seasoning, adjusting if necessary, and serve with warm crusty bread, if desired.

Farmhouse Paté

6 THIN SLICES PARMA HAM

2 TABLESPOONS BUTTER

1 ONION, FINELY CHOPPED

1 GARLIC CLOVE, CRUSHED

1/2 CUP CHOPPED MUSHROOMS

8 OUNCES CHICKEN LIVERS,
TRIMMED AND DICED

8 OUNCES SKINLESS
CHICKEN FILLET, DICED

8 OUNCES GROUND PORK

4 OUNCES BACON, DICED

2 TABLESPOONS BRANDY

2 TABLESPOONS GREEN
PEPPERCORNS IN BRINE, DRAINED

4 TEASPOONS CHOPPED
FRESH THYME

SALT AND GROUND BLACK PEPPER

FRESH HERB SPRIGS, TO GARNISH

CRUSTY FRENCH BREAD,
TO SERVE

◆ Line the bottom and sides of a 5-cup ovenproof dish with Parma ham, allowing edges to hang over sides.

◆ Melt butter in a pan, add onion, garlic, and mushrooms and sauté 5 minutes. Add chicken livers, chicken fillet, pork, and bacon and cook until meat is colored all over, stirring frequently. Cool slightly.

◆ Grind in a blender or food processor with brandy. Transfer to a bowl and stir in peppercorns, chopped thyme, and seasoning. Mix well. Spoon into prepared dish and press down lightly, leveling the surface.

◆ Fold Parma ham over the top, then cover with aluminum foil. Place in the cooking pot of the slow cooker. Add sufficient boiling water to the cooking pot to come halfway up the sides of the dish.

◆ Cover and cook on HIGH 5 to 6 hours, or until cooked and the juices of the paté run clear when pierced with a skewer.

◆ Lift out, remove foil, drain off any excess juices, and let cool. Chill before serving.

◆ Turn out onto a serving plate and garnish with fresh herb sprigs. Serve with crusty French bread.

Chicken Liver Paté

MAKES 6 TO 8 SERVINGS

6 SLICES BACON

3 TABLESPOONS BUTTER

1 ONION, FINELY CHOPPED

2 GARLIC CLOVES, CRUSHED

*1 POUND CHICKEN LIVERS,
TRIMMED AND HALVED*

2 TABLESPOONS RUBY PORT

2 TABLESPOONS THICK CREAM

*1½ TEASPOONS
DRIED MIXED HERBS*

SALT AND GROUND BLACK PEPPER

MIXED SALAD LEAVES, TO GARNISH

*TOAST OR WARM CRUSTY BREAD,
TO SERVE*

◆ Stretch bacon slices using the back of a knife. Line the bottom and sides of a 6-inch round ovenproof dish with the bacon. Set aside.

◆ Melt butter in a pan, add onion and garlic, and cook gently 5 minutes, stirring occasionally. Add chicken livers and cook about 5 minutes, or until sealed all over, stirring occasionally.

◆ Remove pan from the heat, cool slightly, then stir in port, cream, dried herbs, and seasoning. Purée mixture in a blender or food processor until smooth. Spoon into the prepared dish and level the surface. Cover with aluminum foil.

◆ Place in the cooking pot of the slow cooker and add sufficient boiling water to the cooking pot to come halfway up the sides of the dish. Cover and cook on HIGH 5 to 6 hours, or until thoroughly cooked. Lift out, remove foil, and let cool. Chill before serving.

◆ Turn out onto a serving plate and garnish with salad leaves. Serve with toast or warm crusty bread.

Eggplant Dip

MAKES 6 TO 8 SERVINGS

2 MEDIUM EGGPLANTS

¼ CUP OLIVE OIL

6 SHALLOTS, FINELY CHOPPED

2 GARLIC CLOVES, CRUSHED

1 CUP CHOPPED LARGE FLAT
(FIELD) MUSHROOMS

1½ TEASPOONS
GROUND CORIANDER

1½ TEASPOONS GROUND CUMIN

¼ CUP DRY WHITE WINE

SALT AND GROUND BLACK PEPPER

¼ CUP CHOPPED FRESH CILANTRO

BREADSTICKS, VEGETABLE
CRUDITÉS OR TOASTED ITALIAN
BREAD, TO SERVE

◆ Trim and dice eggplants. Set aside. Heat oil in a large pan, add shallots and garlic, and sauté 3 minutes. Add eggplants and mushrooms and cook 10 to 15 minutes, or until soft, stirring occasionally.

◆ Add coriander and cumin and cook 1 minute, stirring. Remove pan from the heat and let cool slightly.

◆ Place mixture in a blender or food processor with wine and seasoning and blend until smooth and well mixed.

◆ Transfer mixture to the cooking pot in the slow cooker and level the surface. Cover and cook on LOW 4 to 5 hours.

◆ Stir in chopped cilantro and serve with breadsticks, vegetable crudités, or toasted Italian bread.

Variation
Cool and chill before serving. If serving cold, stir 4 to 6 tablespoons thick soured cream into the dip just before serving, if desired.

Fish

Rosemary-Baked Mackerel

1 SMALL ONION, THINLY SLICED

*1 EATING APPLE,
CORED AND THINLY SLICED*

*2 OR 3 TOMATOES,
PEELED AND SLICED*

⅔ CUP FISH OR CHICKEN STOCK

SMALL FRESH ROSEMARY SPRIG

DASH WORCESTERSHIRE SAUCE

SALT AND GROUND BLACK PEPPER

*4 MACKEREL FILLETS, EACH
WEIGHING 6 TO 8 OUNCES*

◆ Preheat the slow cooker on HIGH while preparing ingredients. Place onion, apple, tomatoes, and stock in a saucepan. Add rosemary and Worcestershire sauce and season with salt and pepper. Bring to a boil, then cover and simmer 5 minutes.

◆ Fold mackerel fillets in half with skin side outermost and place in the cooking pot. Pour sauce over fish.

◆ Cover, reduce temperature to LOW, and cook 2 to 3 hours, or until fish is cooked.

Mackerel with Soured Cream

MAKES 4 SERVINGS

2 TABLESPOONS BUTTER

1 LEEK, THINLY SLICED

8-OUNCE CAN CHOPPED TOMATOES

2 TABLESPOONS VEGETABLE STOCK
OR DRY WHITE WINE

1 TABLESPOON CHOPPED FRESH DILL

1/2 TEASPOON MILD PAPRIKA

JUICE 1/2 LEMON

SALT AND GROUND BLACK PEPPER

4 MACKEREL FILLETS,
EACH WEIGHING ABOUT 4 OUNCES

2/3 CUP THICK SOURED CREAM

DILL SPRIGS, TO GARNISH

◆ Preheat the slow cooker on HIGH while preparing ingredients. Melt butter in a saucepan, add leek, and sauté 5 minutes. Add tomatoes, stock or wine, chopped dill, paprika, lemon juice, and seasoning and bring to a boil.

◆ Place mackerel fillets in the cooking pot, skin side down. Pour leek and tomato sauce over fish. Cover, reduce temperature to LOW, and cook 3 to 4 hours, or until fish is cooked.

◆ Drizzle over soured cream, garnish with dill sprigs, and serve. Serve with cooked fresh vegetables, such as snow peas, if desired.

Fish Couscous

2 POUNDS WHITE FISH FILLETS, SKINNED AND CUT INTO SMALL CHUNKS

3 TABLESPOONS OLIVE OIL

1 LARGE ONION, FINELY CHOPPED

2 GARLIC CLOVES, CHOPPED

1 TABLESPOON CHOPPED FRESH THYME

2 CARROTS, FINELY CHOPPED

4 OUNCES BUTTON MUSHROOMS

1¼ CUPS PASSATA

14-OUNCE CAN CHICKPEAS, DRAINED

⅓ CUP RAISINS

½ CUP CASHEWS, TOASTED

1¾ CUPS COUSCOUS

2 TABLESPOONS CHOPPED FRESH PARSLEY

SALT AND GROUND BLACK PEPPER

SPICE MIX

1 TABLESPOON CORIANDER SEEDS, TOASTED

1 TABLESPOON CUMIN SEEDS, TOASTED

2 TEASPOONS CINNAMON

2 TEASPOONS TURMERIC

GRATED ZEST AND JUICE ½ LEMON

2 TEASPOONS HARISSA PASTE

3 TABLESPOONS EXTRA VIRGIN OLIVE OIL

◆ To make spice mix, using a mortar and pestle, combine toasted coriander and cumin seeds, cinnamon, turmeric, lemon zest and juice, harissa paste, and olive oil and grind to make a smooth paste.

◆ Wash and dry fish and place in a non-metallic dish. Add 2 tablespoons of spice mix and turn fish to coat thoroughly. Cover dish and place in the refrigerator to marinate several hours, or overnight if possible.

◆ Preheat the slow cooker on HIGH while preparing ingredients. Heat oil in a large saucepan and sauté onion, garlic, thyme, carrots, and mushrooms 10 minutes, or until softened. Add 1 tablespoon spice mix and sauté an additional 1 minute. Stir in passata and chickpeas and bring to a boil.

◆ Stir in raisins, cashews, and marinated fish. Transfer to cooking pot, cover, reduce temperature to LOW, and cook 2 to 4 hours, or until fish and vegetables are cooked and tender.

◆ Meanwhile, wash couscous with cold water and spread out over a large baking tray. Pour over 2 cups water and let soak 20 minutes.

◆ Steam couscous, either in a double boiler, or in a muslin-lined steamer 8 to 10 minutes until fluffed up and tender.

◆ Sprinkle parsley over fish stew and season to taste. Spoon couscous onto a serving plate and top with fish stew. Serve.

Tuna, Tomato and Olive Casserole

2 TABLESPOONS OLIVE OIL

1 RED ONION, THINLY SLICED

1 YELLOW BELL PEPPER, SEEDED AND THINLY SLICED

2 GARLIC CLOVES, CRUSHED

2 TABLESPOONS ALL-PURPOSE FLOUR

1 CUP FISH OR VEGETABLE STOCK

⅔ CUP RED OR DRY WHITE WINE

5 OR 6 PLUM TOMATOES, PEELED AND CHOPPED

8 OUNCES BUTTON MUSHROOMS, HALVED

2 ZUCCHINI, SLICED

SALT AND GROUND BLACK PEPPER

14-OUNCE CAN TUNA IN BRINE OR SPRING WATER

12-OUNCE CAN CORN KERNELS, DRAINED

¾ CUP PITTED BLACK OLIVES

2 TABLESPOONS CHOPPED FRESH MIXED HERBS

COOKED PASTA, SUCH AS FUSILLI OR PENNE, TO SERVE

Variations
Use canned salmon in place of tuna. Use 14-ounce can chickpeas, rinsed and drained, in place of corn.

◆ Preheat slow cooker on HIGH while preparing ingredients. Heat oil in a pan, add onion, bell pepper, and garlic and sauté 5 minutes.

◆ Stir in flour and cook 1 minute, stirring. Gradually stir in stock and wine, then add tomatoes, mushrooms, zucchini, and seasoning and bring to a boil, stirring.

◆ Transfer to the cooking pot, cover and cook on HIGH 3 to 4 hours.

◆ Drain and flake tuna. Stir tuna, corn, and olives into vegetable sauce. Cover and cook on HIGH an additional 1 to 2 hours, or until casserole is piping hot.

◆ Stir in chopped fresh mixed herbs and serve with cooked pasta, such as fusilli or penne.

Salmon and Broccoli Risotto

MAKES 4 SERVINGS

2 TABLESPOONS BUTTER

6 SHALLOTS, THINLY SLICED

2 GARLIC CLOVES, CRUSHED

1 RED BELL PEPPER, SEEDED AND DICED

1 CUP SLICED CHESTNUT MUSHROOMS

1¼ CUPS EASY-COOK RISOTTO RICE OR AMERICAN EASY-COOK LONG-GRAIN RICE

3¾ CUPS DRY WHITE WINE

2 TO 2½ CUPS FISH OR VEGETABLE STOCK

SALT AND GROUND BLACK PEPPER

1 CUP SMALL BROCCOLI FLORETS, CUT IN HALF

14 OUNCES SKINLESS BONELESS COOKED SALMON, FLAKED

2 TABLESPOONS CHOPPED FRESH FLAT-LEAF PARSLEY

FRESH PARMESAN CHEESE SHAVINGS, TO SERVE

Variation
Use 14-ounce can pink or red salmon, drained, boned, and flaked, in place of cooked fresh salmon.

◆ Preheat the slow cooker on HIGH while preparing ingredients. Melt butter in a pan, add shallots, garlic, bell pepper, and mushrooms and sauté 5 minutes.

◆ Add rice and cook 1 minute, stirring. Stir in wine, 2 cups stock, and seasoning and bring to a boil.

◆ Transfer to the cooking pot, cover, and cook on HIGH 1 to 2 hours, or until rice is just tender and most of the liquid has been absorbed.

◆ Meanwhile, cook broccoli in a pan of boiling water about 5 minutes or until just tender. Drain well.

◆ Stir broccoli and salmon into risotto, adding a little extra hot stock if required. Cover and cook on HIGH about 30 minutes.

◆ Stir in chopped parsley, serve in individual dishes, and sprinkle with Parmesan shavings.

Sicilian Salt Cod

2 POUNDS SALT COD

MILK

¼ CUP SEASONED
ALL-PURPOSE FLOUR

¼ CUP OLIVE OIL

8 BABY ONIONS, HALVED

2 GARLIC CLOVES, CHOPPED

4 RIPE TOMATOES, CHOPPED

⅔ CUP GOLDEN RAISINS

½ CUP PITTED OLIVES, HALVED

2 TABLESPOONS BALSAMIC VINEGAR

⅔ CUP CHICKEN OR
VEGETABLE STOCK

2 TABLESPOONS TOMATO PASTE

1 TEASPOON SUGAR

PEPPER

2 TABLESPOONS CHOPPED
FRESH PARSLEY

◆ Wash salt cod, place in a bowl, and cover with cold water. Let soak 12 hours, changing water several times if possible.

◆ Drain fish, rinse under cold running water, and pat dry. Remove skin and cut flesh into small chunks. Place in a shallow dish, cover with milk, and let soak an additional 2 hours. Wash fish again, pat dry, and dust lightly in seasoned flour.

◆ Preheat the slow cooker on HIGH. Heat half the oil in a non-stick skillet. Add cod and cook 3 minutes, until sealed all over. Remove with a slotted spoon and set aside.

◆ Add remaining oil to the pan and sauté onions and garlic about 5 minutes, or until softened. Add tomatoes, golden raisins, olives, vinegar, stock, tomato paste, sugar, and pepper. Bring to a boil, then stir in cod. Transfer to the cooking pot, cover, reduce temperature to LOW, and cook 2 to 4 hours, or until fish and vegetables are cooked.

◆ Sprinkle with parsley and serve with rice, pasta or bread, if desired.

Poultry
and Game

Italian Chicken Cassoulet

MAKES 6 SERVINGS

1 CUP DRIED BLACK-EYE
OR CRANBERRY BEANS,
SOAKED OVERNIGHT

2 TABLESPOONS OLIVE OIL

4 CHICKEN PORTIONS, SKINNED

2 LARGE RED ONIONS,
THINLY SLICED

2 GARLIC CLOVES, CRUSHED

2 RED BELL PEPPERS,
SEEDED AND DICED

2 TABLESPOONS ALL-PURPOSE FLOUR

1 CUP CHICKEN STOCK

⅔ CUP RED WINE

14-OUNCE CAN CHOPPED TOMATOES

1 CUP SLICED MUSHROOMS

1 TABLESPOON CHOPPED
FRESH THYME

1 TABLESPOON CHOPPED
FRESH OREGANO

SALT AND GROUND
BLACK PEPPER

FRESH HERB SPRIGS,
TO GARNISH

◆ Preheat the slow cooker on HIGH while preparing ingredients. Drain beans, place in a large pan, cover with fresh cold water, and bring to a boil. Boil 10 minutes, then rinse, drain, and set aside.

◆ Meanwhile, heat oil in a large pan, add chicken portions, and cook until lightly browned all over, turning occasionally. Transfer to the cooking pot and set aside.

◆ Add onions, garlic, and bell peppers to the pan and sauté 5 minutes. Stir in flour and cook 1 minute, stirring. Gradually stir in stock and wine, then add beans, tomatoes, mushrooms, herbs, and seasoning.

◆ Bring to a boil, stirring, then pour over chicken in the cooking pot. Cover and cook on HIGH 2 hours.

◆ Reduce temperature to LOW and cook an additional 4 to 6 hours, or until chicken is cooked and tender.

◆ Garnish chicken with fresh herb sprigs and serve with warm ciabatta bread and a mixed green salad, if desired.

Fragrant Chicken Curry

3 TABLESPOONS SUNFLOWER OIL

2 ONIONS, CHOPPED

4 CARROTS, THINLY SLICED

2 GARLIC CLOVES, CRUSHED

1 FRESH GREEN CHILE, SEEDED AND FINELY CHOPPED

1-INCH PIECE FRESH GINGER, PEELED AND FINELY CHOPPED

2 TABLESPOONS ALL-PURPOSE FLOUR

2 TEASPOONS TURMERIC

2 TEASPOONS GROUND CORIANDER

2 TEASPOONS GROUND CUMIN

SALT AND GROUND BLACK PEPPER

1½ POUNDS SKINLESS BONELESS CHICKEN THIGHS, DICED

1¼ CUPS CHICKEN STOCK

⅔ CUP PASSATA

½ CUP GOLDEN RAISINS

½ CUP TOASTED CASHEWS

2 TO 3 TABLESPOONS CHOPPED FRESH CILANTRO

◆ Preheat the slow cooker on HIGH while preparing ingredients. Heat 1 tablespoon oil in a pan, add onions, carrots, garlic, chile, and ginger and sauté 5 minutes. Transfer to the cooking pot and set aside.

◆ In a small bowl, combine flour, turmeric, coriander, cumin, and salt and pepper. Toss chicken in spiced flour until coated all over.

◆ Heat remaining oil in the pan, add chicken in batches, and cook quickly until sealed all over. Transfer to the cooking pot.

◆ Add stock and passata to pan and bring to boil, stirring and scraping up sediments in the pan. Add to the cooking pot and stir to mix well. Cover cooking pot, reduce temperature to LOW, and cook 6 hours.

◆ Stir in golden raisins, cover, and cook on LOW an additional 1 to 2 hours, or until chicken is cooked and tender.

◆ Stir in cashews and chopped cilantro. Serve with plain boiled rice and a mixed leaf salad, if desired.

Chicken Tagine with Figs, Olives and Pistachio Nuts

MAKES 4 SERVINGS

2 TABLESPOONS OLIVE OIL

8 CHICKEN THIGHS, SKINNED

2 ONIONS, CHOPPED

2 CARROTS, THINLY SLICED

2 GARLIC CLOVES, CRUSHED

2 TEASPOONS GRATED
FRESH GINGER

6 OUNCES BUTTON MUSHROOMS,
HALVED

8 LARGE DRIED FIGS,
ROUGHLY CHOPPED

2 TABLESPOONS ALL-PURPOSE FLOUR

1¾ CUPS CHICKEN STOCK

2 TABLESPOONS TOMATO PASTE

1 TABLESPOON LEMON JUICE

¾ CUP PITTED BLACK OLIVES

⅓ CUP PISTACHIO NUTS
OR PINE NUTS

CHOPPED FRESH PARSLEY,
TO GARNISH

SPICE MIX

2 TABLESPOONS OLIVE OIL

2 TEASPOONS GROUND CORIANDER

2 TEASPOONS GROUND CUMIN

1½ TEASPOONS GROUND CINNAMON

1½ TEASPOONS TURMERIC

FINELY GRATED ZEST AND
JUICE ½ LEMON

1½ TEASPOONS HARISSA PASTE

◆ To make spice mix, combine olive oil, coriander, cumin, cinnamon, turmeric, lemon zest and juice, and harissa paste in a small bowl. Toss chicken thighs in spice mix until coated all over.

◆ Preheat the slow cooker on HIGH. Heat oil in a pan, add chicken, and cook until lightly browned all over, turning occasionally. Transfer to the cooking pot using a slotted spoon. Set aside.

◆ Add onions, carrots, garlic, and ginger to the pan and sauté about 5 minutes, or until slightly softened.

◆ Add mushrooms and figs, then stir in flour and cook 1 minute, stirring. Gradually stir in stock, then add tomato paste and lemon juice. Bring slowly to a boil, stirring, then pour over chicken in the cooking pot. Stir gently to mix.

◆ Cover cooking pot and cook chicken on HIGH 3 to 5 hours until cooked and tender.

◆ About 1 hour before serving, stir olives and nuts into chicken. Serve garnished with parsley and with couscous or rice.

Chicken Cacciatore

MAKES 4 SERVINGS

2 TABLESPOONS OLIVE OIL

*4 SKINLESS CHICKEN BREASTS,
WITH BONES*

1 RED ONION, THINLY SLICED

2 GARLIC CLOVES, THINLY SLICED

*1 RED BELL PEPPER,
SEEDED AND SLICED*

*1 YELLOW BELL PEPPER,
SEEDED AND SLICED*

2 TABLESPOONS ALL-PURPOSE FLOUR

⅔ CUP RED WINE

⅔ CUP CHICKEN STOCK

14-OUNCE CAN CHOPPED TOMATOES

1 TABLESPOON TOMATO PASTE

SALT AND GROUND BLACK PEPPER

PINCH SUGAR

*2 TABLESPOONS CHOPPED
FRESH BASIL*

◆ Preheat the slow cooker on HIGH while preparing ingredients. In a pan, heat oil and fry chicken breasts all over until golden brown, then transfer to the cooking pot using a slotted spoon.

◆ Gently sauté onion, garlic, and bell peppers in pan 5 minutes without browning. Stir in flour and cook 1 minute, stirring.

◆ Add wine, stock, tomatoes, tomato paste, salt and pepper, and sugar and bring to a boil.

◆ Pour over chicken in cooking pot, cover, and cook on HIGH 3 to 5 hours, or until chicken is cooked and tender.

◆ Serve on a bed of pasta noodles, if desired, and sprinkle with basil and plenty of black pepper.

Coq au Vin

2 TABLESPOONS BUTTER

4 CHICKEN JOINTS, SKINNED

12 OUNCES SHALLOTS OR
BUTTON ONIONS

2 GARLIC CLOVES, CRUSHED

3 MEDIUM CARROTS, THINLY SLICED

6 OUNCES LEAN SMOKED BACON,
DICED

¼ CUP ALL-PURPOSE FLOUR

1 CUP CHICKEN STOCK

1 CUP RED WINE

2 TABLESPOONS TOMATO PASTE

8 OUNCES BUTTON MUSHROOMS

SALT AND GROUND BLACK PEPPER

1 BOUQUET GARNI

FRESH HERB SPRIGS, TO GARNISH

◆ Preheat the slow cooker on HIGH while preparing ingredients. Melt butter in a pan. Add chicken portions and cook until lightly browned all over, turning occasionally. Transfer to the cooking pot using a slotted spoon and set aside.

◆ Add shallots or button onions, garlic, carrots, and bacon and sauté 5 minutes. Stir in flour and cook 1 minute, stirring. Gradually stir in stock and wine, then bring to a boil, stirring.

◆ Add tomato paste, mushrooms, seasoning, and bouquet garni and pour over chicken in cooking pot. Cover and cook on HIGH 3 to 5 hours, or until chicken is cooked and tender.

◆ Remove and discard bouquet garni. Garnish chicken with fresh herb sprigs. Serve with plain boiled rice or with boiled egg noodles tossed in melted butter, if desired.

Chicken with Shallots

1 TABLESPOON OLIVE OIL

2 TABLESPOONS BUTTER

4 CHICKEN PORTIONS, SKINNED

1 POUND SHALLOTS, HALVED

2 GARLIC CLOVES, THINLY SLICED

6 OUNCES LEAN BACON, DICED

2 TABLESPOONS ALL-PURPOSE FLOUR

1 CUP DRY WHITE OR ROSÉ WINE

1 CUP CHICKEN STOCK

6 OUNCES BUTTON MUSHROOMS

1 TABLESPOON WHOLEGRAIN MUSTARD

2 BAY LEAVES

SALT AND GROUND BLACK PEPPER

2 TABLESPOONS CHOPPED FRESH FLAT-LEAF PARSLEY

◆ Preheat the slow cooker on HIGH while preparing ingredients. Heat oil and butter in a pan, add chicken, and cook until lightly browned all over. Transfer to the cooking pot using a slotted spoon and set aside.

◆ Add shallots, garlic, and bacon to the pan and sauté 5 minutes. Stir in flour and cook 1 minute, stirring. Gradually stir in wine and stock, then bring to a boil, stirring.

◆ Add mushrooms, mustard, bay leaves, and seasoning, then pour over chicken in the cooking pot. Cover and cook on HIGH 3 to 5 hours, or until chicken is cooked and tender.

◆ Remove and discard bay leaves. Sprinkle with parsley. Serve with mustard-flavored mashed potatoes and green cabbage, if desired.

Variations
Use button onions in place of shallots. Use Dijon-style mustard in place of wholegrain mustard.

Moroccan Chicken Casserole

3½-POUND CHICKEN, CUT INTO 8
PIECES AND SKINNED

¼ CUP LEMON JUICE

5 TABLESPOONS VIRGIN OLIVE OIL

1 TABLESPOON
FINELY CHOPPED GARLIC

1 TEASPOON GROUND GINGER

1 TEASPOON CUMIN

1 TEASPOON GROUND CORIANDER

1 TEASPOON CINNAMON

LARGE PINCH SAFFRON THREADS

½ TEASPOON GROUND BLACK PEPPER

1 ONION, THINLY SLICED

2 TABLESPOONS ALL-PURPOSE FLOUR

2 CUPS CHICKEN STOCK

1 CUP READY-TO-EAT DRIED PRUNES

SMALL BUNCH CILANTRO LEAVES

◆ Place chicken pieces in a large non-metallic dish and sprinkle over lemon juice, 3 tablespoons oil, and garlic. Marinate 2 to 4 hours.

◆ Preheat the slow cooker on HIGH. Remove chicken from marinade using a slotted spoon and reserve marinade. Heat remaining oil in a large pan, add chicken portions, and cook until lightly browned all over. Add ginger, cumin, coriander, cinnamon, saffron threads, and pepper and cook 1 minute. Transfer to cooking pot using a slotted spoon.

◆ Add onion to pan and sauté 5 minutes, then add flour and cook 1 minute, stirring. Stir in stock and reserved marinade, then bring to a boil, stirring. Pour over chicken.

◆ Cover and cook on HIGH 3 to 5 hours, or until chicken is cooked and tender. About 1 hour before serving, stir in prunes.

◆ Shred cilantro leaves and sprinkle over casserole. Serve with steamed couscous, if desired.

Lemon-baked Chicken

MAKES 4 SERVINGS

2 LEMONS

3-POUND OVEN-READY CHICKEN

1 SMALL ONION, QUARTERED

2 TABLESPOONS OLIVE OIL

¾ STICK BUTTER

2 GARLIC CLOVES, THINLY SLICED

¼ CUP BRANDY

2 TABLESPOONS CHOPPED
FRESH FLAT-LEAF PARSLEY

FRESH FLAT-LEAF PARSLEY SPRIGS,
TO GARNISH

◆ Preheat the slow cooker on HIGH while preparing ingredients. Cut 1 lemon into quarters and push into cavity of chicken, together with onion quarters.

◆ Heat oil and butter in a skillet and quickly brown chicken all over. Transfer chicken to cooking pot using a slotted spoon. Set aside.

◆ Grate zest of remaining lemon and add to the pan with garlic. Sauté 3 minutes. Squeeze juice from lemon and add to pan with brandy and chopped parsley.

◆ Bring gently to a boil, stirring. Pour over chicken in the cooking pot, then cover and cook on HIGH 4 to 6 hours, or until chicken is cooked and tender.

◆ Carve chicken and serve with juices spooned over. Garnish with parsley sprigs to serve.

Barbecued Chicken

MAKES 4 SERVINGS

3 *TABLESPOONS BUTTER*

8 *CHICKEN DRUMSTICKS, SKINNED*

2 *RED ONIONS, THINLY SLICED*

2 *TABLESPOONS ALL-PURPOSE FLOUR*

1¼ *CUPS CHICKEN STOCK*

2 *TABLESPOONS TOMATO PASTE*

¼ *CUP RED WINE VINEGAR*

¼ *CUP WORCESTERSHIRE SAUCE*

1 *TABLESPOON MUSTARD POWDER*

SALT AND GROUND BLACK PEPPER

FRESH HERB SPRIGS, TO GARNISH

◆ Preheat the slow cooker on HIGH while preparing ingredients. Melt butter in a pan, add chicken drumsticks and cook until lightly browned all over, turning occasionally. Transfer to the cooking pot using a slotted spoon and set aside.

◆ Add onions to pan and sauté gently 10 minutes. Stir in flour and cook 1 minute, stirring. Gradually stir in stock, then add tomato paste, vinegar, Worcestershire sauce, mustard powder, and seasoning.

◆ Bring to a boil, stirring, then pour over chicken in the cooking pot. Cover and cook on HIGH 3 to 5 hours, or until chicken is cooked and tender.

◆ Garnish with fresh herb sprigs and serve with roast baby new potatoes and a mixed green salad, if desired.

Chicken with Potatoes, Tomatoes and Fennel

MAKES 4 SERVINGS

2 TABLESPOONS OLIVE OIL

4 CHICKEN DRUMSTICKS, SKINNED

4 CHICKEN THIGHS, SKINNED

2 OUNCES THICK-CUT BACON, DICED

2 SMALL FENNEL BULBS,
CUT INTO WEDGES, FEATHERY
FRONDS RESERVED

3 MEDIUM POTATOES,
PEELED AND THINLY SLICED

1 SMALL GARLIC CLOVE,
FINELY CHOPPED

2 TABLESPOONS ALL-PURPOSE FLOUR

2 CUPS CHICKEN STOCK, OR 1 CUP
EACH CHICKEN STOCK AND DRY
WHITE WINE

1½ TEASPOONS CHOPPED
FRESH THYME

1 TEASPOON GRATED LEMON ZEST

SALT AND GROUND BLACK PEPPER

2 OR 3 WELL-FLAVORED
RIPE TOMATOES, QUARTERED

2 TABLESPOONS CHOPPED
FRESH PARSLEY AND RESERVED
FENNEL FRONDS

◆ Preheat the slow cooker on HIGH while preparing ingredients. Heat 1 tablespoon oil in a large pan, add chicken drumsticks and thighs, and fry until lightly browned all over. Transfer to the cooking pot using a slotted spoon.

◆ Heat remaining oil in the pan, add bacon, fennel, potatoes, and garlic and sauté 5 minutes. Stir in flour and cook 1 minute, stirring. Stir in stock, and wine if using, and bring to a boil, stirring.

◆ Pour over chicken in cooking pot, add thyme, lemon zest, and seasoning and stir to mix. Tuck tomatoes around and between chicken pieces.

◆ Cover and cook on HIGH 4 to 6 hours, or until chicken and vegetables are cooked and tender.

◆ Mix together parsley and fennel fronds and sprinkle over casserole to serve. Serve with mashed potatoes and fresh peas, if desired.

Country Chicken Casserole

2 TABLESPOONS BUTTER

4 SKINLESS CHICKEN FILLETS, EACH
CUT INTO 3 PIECES

12 OUNCES BUTTON ONIONS OR
SHALLOTS

2 LEEKS, THINLY SLICED

2 STALKS CELERY, THINLY SLICED

8 OUNCES BABY CARROTS

8 OUNCES BUTTON MUSHROOMS

1/3 CUP PEARL BARLEY

14-OUNCE CAN CHOPPED TOMATOES

2 TABLESPOONS TOMATO PASTE

1 CUP CHICKEN STOCK

1 CUP DRY WHITE WINE

SALT AND GROUND BLACK PEPPER

1 BOUQUET GARNI

FRESH HERB SPRIGS, TO GARNISH

◆ Preheat the slow cooker on HIGH while preparing ingredients. Melt butter in a pan, add chicken, and cook until lightly browned all over, stirring occasionally. Transfer to the cooking pot using a slotted spoon and set aside.

◆ Add onions or shallots, leeks, celery, carrots, and mushrooms and sauté 5 minutes. Stir in pearl barley, tomatoes, tomato paste, stock, wine, and seasoning, then bring to a boil.

◆ Add bouquet garni, then pour over chicken in the cooking pot. Cover, reduce the temperature to LOW, and cook 8 to 10 hours, or until chicken is cooked and tender.

◆ Garnish with fresh herb sprigs and serve with mashed potatoes and green beans, if desired.

Variation
Use small turkey breast steaks in place of chicken fillets.

Poussins Braised in Wine

MAKES 4 SERVINGS

4 POUSSINS, EACH WEIGHING ABOUT 12 OUNCES

1 LEMON, CUT INTO QUARTERS

FEW SPRIGS FRESH CILANTRO

3 TABLESPOONS BUTTER

2 LEEKS, SLICED

⅔ CUP RED WINE

2 TABLESPOONS CLEAR HONEY

SALT AND GROUND BLACK PEPPER

1 TABLESPOON CORNSTARCH

FRESH CILANTRO SPRIGS, TO GARNISH

◆ Preheat the slow cooker on HIGH while preparing ingredients. Stuff each poussin with one quarter of lemon and 1 or 2 sprigs of cilantro.

◆ Melt butter in a skillet and quickly brown birds all over. Transfer them to the cooking pot, using a slotted spoon. Set aside.

◆ Add leeks to pan and sauté 5 minutes. Add wine, honey, and seasoning and bring to a boil, stirring. Pour over poussins.

◆ Cover the cooking pot and cook on HIGH 4 to 6 hours, or until poussins are cooked and tender. Remove poussins from the cooking pot, place on a plate, and keep hot.

◆ In a small pan, blend cornstarch with a little water. Stir in red wine sauce from the cooking pot, then bring to a boil, stirring, until thickened. Simmer gently 3 minutes, stirring.

◆ Serve poussins with wine and leek sauce spooned over. Garnish with fresh cilantro sprigs and serve with creamy mashed potatoes and stir-fried green vegetables, if desired.

Curried Turkey with Coconut

2 TABLESPOONS OLIVE OIL

1 ONION, CHOPPED

2 GARLIC CLOVES, CRUSHED

1 GREEN BELL PEPPER, SEEDED
AND THINLY SLICED

18 OUNCES SKINLESS
BONELESS TURKEY MEAT,
CUT INTO SMALL DICE

1 TEASPOON GROUND CORIANDER

1 TEASPOON GROUND CUMIN

4 TEASPOONS THAI GREEN
CURRY PASTE

8 OUNCES GREEN BEANS, HALVED

6 OUNCES BABY CORN, HALVED

1¼ CUPS CHICKEN STOCK

⅔ CUP COCONUT MILK

2 TABLESPOONS CORNSTARCH

2 OR 3 TABLESPOONS CHOPPED
FRESH CILANTRO

TOASTED FLAKED COCONUT,
TO GARNISH

◆ Preheat the slow cooker on HIGH while preparing ingredients. Heat oil in a pan, add onion, garlic, bell pepper, and turkey and sauté about 5 minutes, or until turkey is sealed all over, stirring occasionally.

◆ Add coriander, cumin, and curry paste and cook 1 minute, stirring. Add beans, corn, stock, and coconut milk and stir to mix.

◆ In a small bowl, blend cornstarch with a little water, add to curry and stir well to mix. Bring to a boil, stirring, then transfer to cooking pot.

◆ Cover, reduce the temperature to LOW, and cook 6 to 8 hours, or until turkey is cooked and tender.

◆ Stir in chopped cilantro and garnish with toasted flaked coconut. Serve with plain boiled rice, if desired.

Braised Duck with Orange

MAKES 4 SERVINGS

2 TABLESPOONS BUTTER

4 DUCK PORTIONS, SKINNED

2 RED ONIONS, THINLY SLICED

1 CUP SLICED CHESTNUT
MUSHROOMS

2 TABLESPOONS ALL-PURPOSE FLOUR

SEEDS FROM 4 CARDAMOM PODS,
CRUSHED

¾ CUP CHICKEN STOCK

⅔ CUP RED WINE

GRATED ZEST AND JUICE 1 ORANGE

2 TABLESPOONS ORANGE MARMALADE

SALT AND GROUND BLACK PEPPER

FRESH HERB SPRIGS, TO GARNISH

◆ Preheat the slow cooker on HIGH while preparing ingredients. Melt butter in a pan. Add duck and cook until lightly browned all over, turning occasionally. Transfer to the cooking pot using a slotted spoon and set aside.

◆ Add onions and mushrooms to the pan and sauté 5 minutes. Stir in flour and cardamom and cook 1 minute, stirring. Gradually stir in stock and wine, then add orange zest and juice, marmalade, and seasoning.

◆ Bring to boil, stirring, then pour over duck in the cooking pot. Cover and cook on HIGH 3 to 5 hours, or until duck is cooked and tender.

◆ Garnish with fresh herb sprigs and serve with boiled new potatoes, snow peas and baby corn, if desired.

Variation
Use chicken in place of duck portions.

Venison Casserole

MAKES 4 TO 6 SERVINGS

2 TABLESPOONS SUNFLOWER OIL

1½ POUNDS LEAN STEWING VENISON, CUT INTO SMALL DICE

2 RED ONIONS, THINLY SLICED

4 CARROTS, THINLY SLICED

3 STALKS CELERY, THINLY SLICED

3 TABLESPOONS ALL-PURPOSE FLOUR

1 CUP GAME OR CHICKEN STOCK

1 CUP RED WINE

2 TABLESPOONS CRANBERRY SAUCE

1 TABLESPOON CHOPPED FRESH THYME

7 OUNCES BUTTON MUSHROOMS

⅔ CUP DRIED CRANBERRIES

SALT AND GROUND BLACK PEPPER

FRESH HERB SPRIGS, TO GARNISH

Variation
Use lean braising or stewing beef in place of venison.

◆ Preheat the slow cooker on HIGH while preparing ingredients. Heat oil in a large pan, add venison, and cook until sealed all over, stirring occasionally. Transfer to cooking pot using a slotted spoon. Set aside.

◆ Add onions, carrots, and celery to the pan and sauté 5 minutes. Stir in flour and cook 1 minute, stirring. Gradually stir in stock and wine, then add cranberry sauce, chopped thyme, mushrooms, dried cranberries, and seasoning and bring to a boil, stirring.

◆ Transfer to the cooking pot and stir to mix well. Cover, reduce the temperature to LOW, and cook 8 to 10 hours, or until venison is cooked and tender.

◆ Garnish with fresh herb sprigs and serve with mustard-flavored mashed potatoes and broccoli florets, if desired.

Meat

Beef with Raisins and Pine Nuts

MAKES 4 SERVINGS

1/3 CUP OLIVE OIL

2 POUNDS LEAN BRAISING STEAK,
CUT INTO SMALL DICE

1 LARGE ONION, CHOPPED

1 GARLIC CLOVE, CHOPPED

8 OUNCES BUTTON MUSHROOMS,
HALVED IF LARGE

1 RED BELL PEPPER,
SEEDED AND DICED

1 TABLESPOON CHOPPED
FRESH THYME

1 TABLESPOON CHOPPED FRESH
ROSEMARY

2 TABLESPOONS SEASONED
ALL-PURPOSE FLOUR

2 TEASPOONS PAPRIKA

1 TEASPOON CINNAMON

2/3 CUP BEER

14-OUNCE CAN CHOPPED TOMATOES

2 BAY LEAVES

1 CUP BEEF STOCK

1/2 CUP PINE NUTS

1/3 CUP RAISINS

◆ Preheat the slow cooker on HIGH while preparing ingredients. Heat half the oil in a non-stick skillet and fry meat over a medium heat 4 or 5 minutes, until lightly browned. Use a slotted spoon to transfer beef to cooking pot.

◆ Heat remaining oil in pan and sauté onion, garlic, mushrooms, bell pepper, thyme, and rosemary 5 minutes. Stir in flour, paprika, and cinnamon and cook 1 minute, stirring. Stir in beer, then add tomatoes, bay leaves, and stock and bring to a boil, stirring.

◆ Pour over beef in cooking pot and stir to mix. Cover, reduce the temperature to LOW, and cook 7 to 9 hours.

◆ Stir in pine nuts and raisins, cover, and cook on LOW an additional 1 to 2 hours, or until beef is cooked and tender.

◆ Serve with baked potatoes and broccoli florets, if desired.

Beef Tagine with Prunes

MAKES 6 SERVINGS

1¼ CUPS READY-TO-EAT DRIED PRUNES

1 TEASPOON GROUND GINGER

1 TEASPOON GROUND CORIANDER

PINCH SAFFRON THREADS

SALT AND GROUND BLACK PEPPER

3 TABLESPOONS OLIVE OIL

2½ POUNDS LEAN STEWING BEEF, CUT INTO SMALL DICE

2 ONIONS, THINLY SLICED

2 GARLIC CLOVES, CRUSHED

1 TABLESPOON ALL-PURPOSE FLOUR

2 CUPS BEEF STOCK OR WATER

1 CINNAMON STICK

1 TABLESPOON CLEAR HONEY

1 TEASPOON HARISSA PASTE

1 TABLESPOON SESAME SEEDS

3 TABLESPOONS CHOPPED FRESH PARSLEY

1 TEASPOON ORANGE FLOWER WATER, TO SERVE

◆ Place prunes in a bowl and cover with boiling water. Let soak 2 hours.

◆ Preheat the slow cooker on HIGH. In a large bowl, mix together ginger, coriander, saffron, salt and pepper, and 2 tablespoons of olive oil. Add beef and mix well, rubbing spices into meat with your fingers.

◆ In a large skillet, heat remaining oil. Add beef and cook until sealed all over. Transfer to cooking pot using a slotted spoon. Set aside.

◆ Add onions and garlic to pan and sauté 5 minutes. Stir in flour and cook 1 minute, stirring. Stir in stock or water and bring to a boil, stirring, then add cinnamon stick. Pour over beef and stir to mix. Cover, reduce temperature to LOW, and cook 7 to 9 hours.

◆ Drain prunes and stir into beef mixture with honey and harissa paste. Cover and cook on LOW an additional 1 to 2 hours.

◆ Meanwhile, dry-fry sesame seeds until lightly browned.

◆ To serve, stir in parsley, sprinkle with orange flower water, and sprinkle sesame seeds on top. Serve with couscous, if desired.

Beef Goulash with Chile

2 TABLESPOONS OLIVE OIL

*1½ POUNDS LEAN STEWING
OR BRAISING STEAK,
CUT INTO SMALL CUBES*

1 ONION, SLICED

1 GARLIC CLOVE, CRUSHED

*1 POUND POTATOES, PEELED AND
CUT INTO SMALL CUBES*

*2 GREEN BELL PEPPERS, SEEDED
AND THINLY SLICED*

*1 FRESH GREEN CHILE, SEEDED
AND THINLY SLICED*

2 TABLESPOONS ALL-PURPOSE FLOUR

1 TABLESPOON PAPRIKA

1¼ CUPS BEEF STOCK

14-OUNCE CAN CHOPPED TOMATOES

2 TABLESPOONS TOMATO PASTE

PINCH CARAWAY SEEDS

2 BAY LEAVES

SALT AND GROUND BLACK PEPPER

◆ Preheat the slow cooker on HIGH while preparing ingredients. Heat oil in a pan, add beef, and cook until meat is sealed all over, stirring occasionally. Transfer to cooking pot using a slotted spoon. Set aside.

◆ Add onion, garlic, potatoes, bell peppers, and chile to the pan and sauté about 5 minutes, or until slightly softened.

◆ Stir in flour and paprika and cook 1 minute, stirring. Gradually stir in stock, then add tomatoes, tomato paste, caraway seeds, bay leaves, and seasoning and mix well. Bring to a boil, stirring, then transfer to the cooking pot and stir to mix.

◆ Cover, reduce temperature to LOW, and cook 10 to 12 hours, or until beef is cooked and tender.

◆ Remove and discard bay leaves and adjust seasoning. Serve with fresh bread or cooked noodles or rice, if desired.

Curried Pot-roast Beef

MAKES 6 SERVINGS

2 TEASPOONS TURMERIC

2 TEASPOONS GROUND CORIANDER

2 TEASPOONS GROUND CUMIN

1 TEASPOON HOT CHILI POWDER

1 TEASPOON GARAM MASALA

SALT AND GROUND BLACK PEPPER

3-POUND LEAN BEEF JOINT

3 TABLESPOONS SUNFLOWER OIL

8 SHALLOTS, SLICED

4 CARROTS, THINLY SLICED

4 STALKS CELERY, THINLY SLICED

1 RUTABAGA, CUT INTO SMALL DICE

2½ CUPS BEEF STOCK

2 TABLESPOONS CORNSTARCH

◆ Preheat the slow cooker on HIGH while preparing ingredients. In a small bowl, mix together turmeric, coriander, cumin, chili powder, garam masala, salt, and pepper. Rub spice mixture all over beef.

◆ Heat 2 tablespoons oil in a non-stick skillet, add beef, and cook quickly, turning frequently, until lightly browned and sealed all over. Transfer to the cooking pot.

◆ Heat remaining oil in the pan, add shallots, carrots, celery, and rutabaga and sauté 5 minutes. Spoon vegetables around beef. Add stock to the pan, gently scraping up sediments in pan using a wooden spoon and bring to a boil.

◆ Pour enough stock into cooking pot to just cover vegetables. Cover, reduce temperature to LOW, and cook 6 to 8 hours or until beef is cooked and tender, turning beef and stirring once.

◆ Remove beef, place on a plate, cover, and keep hot. Transfer vegetables to a saucepan.

◆ In a small bowl, blend cornstarch with a little water until smooth. Stir into vegetable mixture, then bring to boil, stirring, until thickened. Simmer gently 3 minutes.

◆ Slice beef and spoon vegetables over. Serve with plain boiled rice, if desired.

Beef with Paprika and Potatoes

3 TABLESPOONS OLIVE OIL

1½ POUNDS LEAN STEWING BEEF,
CUT INTO SMALL CUBES

2 ONIONS, CHOPPED

1 GARLIC CLOVE, CRUSHED

1 RED BELL PEPPER, SEEDED
AND THINLY SLICED

3 MEDIUM POTATOES,
PEELED AND DICED

2 TABLESPOONS ALL-PURPOSE FLOUR

2 TABLESPOONS PAPRIKA

2 OR 3 TABLESPOONS
CARAWAY SEEDS

2 TABLESPOONS TOMATO PASTE

1½ CUPS BEEF OR
VEGETABLE STOCK

SALT AND GROUND BLACK PEPPER

⅔ CUP SOURED CREAM

◆ Preheat the slow cooker on HIGH while preparing ingredients. Heat 2 tablespoons oil in a large saucepan, add beef, and cook until sealed all over. Transfer to cooking pot using a slotted spoon.

◆ Heat remaining oil in pan, add onions, garlic, red bell pepper, and potatoes and sauté 5 minutes. Add flour, paprika, and caraway seeds and cook 1 minute, stirring.

◆ Add tomato paste, stock, and seasoning. Bring to a boil, then pour over beef and stir to mix. Cover, reduce temperature to LOW, and cook 10 to 12 hours, or until beef is cooked and tender.

◆ Pour over soured cream and stir to give a marbled effect. Cover and heat through on LOW 20 to 30 minutes. Serve with fresh bread or cooked rice or noodles, if desired.

Pork, Potato and Fennel Casserole

MAKES 6 SERVINGS

2½ POUNDS LEAN PORK TENDERLOIN
OR BONELESS PORK SHOULDER, CUT
INTO SMALL DICE

1 TEASPOON CHOPPED FRESH THYME

1 TEASPOON FENNEL SEEDS,
CRUSHED

2 GARLIC CLOVES, CHOPPED

2 CUPS MEDIUM-BODIED
DRY WHITE WINE

2 FENNEL BULBS

SEASONED ALL-PURPOSE FLOUR

4-OUNCE PIECE PANCETTA,
CUT INTO THIN STRIPS

3 TABLESPOONS VIRGIN OLIVE OIL

2 ONIONS, THINLY SLICED

1½ POUNDS SMALL NEW POTATOES

SALT AND GROUND BLACK PEPPER

TOPPING

1½ TEASPOONS FINELY GRATED
LEMON ZEST

½ GARLIC CLOVE, FINELY CHOPPED

2 TABLESPOONS CHOPPED
FRESH PARSLEY

FEATHERY FENNEL FRONDS,
CHOPPED (SEE METHOD)

◆ Mix pork with thyme, fennel seeds, garlic, and wine in a non-metallic dish. Cover and chill at least 4 hours, or overnight, stirring occasionally.

◆ Preheat the slow cooker on HIGH. Trim and reserve feathery fronds of fennel bulbs, then cut each bulb into 6 wedges. Set aside.

◆ Lift pork from marinade, reserving marinade. Pat pork dry on absorbent kitchen paper and coat lightly with seasoned flour.

◆ Fry pancetta in 2 tablespoons oil in a large pan until lightly browned and fat runs. Transfer to cooking pot using a slotted spoon. Set aside.

◆ Add onions, fennel bulb wedges, and potatoes to pan and sauté 5 minutes. Add to cooking pot.

◆ Add remaining oil to pan, add pork, and cook until sealed all over. Stir in marinade and seasoning, bring to a boil, and bubble 2 minutes.

◆ Transfer pork to cooking pot and stir to mix. Cover the cooking pot, reduce temperature to LOW, and cook 8 to 10 hours, or until pork is cooked and tender.

◆ To make topping, in a small bowl mix together lemon zest, garlic, parsley, and reserved fennel fronds. Sprinkle over casserole to serve. Serve with cooked fresh vegetables such as baby carrots and green beans, if desired.

Braised Pork with Cabbage and Apples

MAKES 4 SERVINGS

1 TABLESPOON OLIVE OIL

2 TABLESPOONS BUTTER

4 LEAN LOIN PORK CHOPS

1 LARGE ONION, THINLY SLICED

3 STALKS CELERY, FINELY CHOPPED

2 TABLESPOONS ALL-PURPOSE FLOUR

1 CUP CHICKEN OR
VEGETABLE STOCK

1 CUP DRY OR MEDIUM CIDER

3 CUPS SHREDDED WHITE CABBAGE

1 LARGE COOKING APPLE, PEELED,
CORED AND SLICED

1 TEASPOON DRIED SAGE

SALT AND GROUND BLACK PEPPER

FRESH HERB SPRIGS, TO GARNISH

Variation
Use fresh or dried thyme in place of dried sage.

◆ Preheat the slow cooker on HIGH while preparing ingredients. Heat oil and butter in a pan. Add chops and cook until sealed all over, turning once. Transfer to the cooking pot using a slotted spoon and set aside.

◆ Add onion and celery to the pan and sauté 5 minutes. Stir in flour and cook 1 minute, stirring. Gradually stir in stock and cider, then bring to a boil, stirring.

◆ Add cabbage, apple, sage, and seasoning and stir to mix. Pour mixture over chops. Cover, reduce the temperature to LOW, and cook 6 to 8 hours, or until pork is cooked and tender.

◆ Garnish with fresh herb sprigs. Serve with mashed potatoes and vegetables such as peas, if desired.

Paprika Pork and Bean Casserole

1¼ CUPS DRIED KIDNEY
OR BLACK-EYE BEANS,
SOAKED OVERNIGHT

3 TABLESPOONS BUTTER

1½ POUNDS LEAN PORK TENDERLOIN
OR BONELESS PORK SHOULDER,
CUT INTO SMALL CUBES

1 ONION, CHOPPED

1 GARLIC CLOVE, CRUSHED

2 LEEKS, THINLY SLICED

2 STALKS CELERY, SLICED

3 CARROTS, THINLY SLICED

¼ CUP ALL-PURPOSE FLOUR

1 TABLESPOON PAPRIKA

1¼ CUPS CHICKEN
OR VEGETABLE STOCK

1 CUP DRY OR MEDIUM CIDER

8-OUNCE CAN CHOPPED TOMATOES

1 TABLESPOON TOMATO PASTE

SALT AND GROUND
BLACK PEPPER

1 BOUQUET GARNI

SOURED CREAM,
TO SERVE (OPTIONAL)

◆ Preheat the slow cooker on HIGH while preparing ingredients. Drain beans, place in a large pan, and cover with fresh cold water. Bring to a boil and boil 10 minutes. Rinse, drain, and set aside.

◆ Meanwhile, melt butter in a pan, add meat, and cook until sealed all over. Transfer to the cooking pot using a slotted spoon and set aside.

◆ Add onion, garlic, leeks, celery, and carrots to the pan and sauté 5 minutes. Stir in flour and paprika and cook 1 minute, stirring. Gradually stir in stock and cider, then add tomatoes, tomato paste, beans, and seasoning.

◆ Bring to a boil, stirring, then add bouquet garni. Transfer to the cooking pot and stir to mix. Cover, reduce the temperature to LOW, and cook 8 to 10 hours, or until pork is cooked and tender.

◆ Remove and discard bouquet garni. Top each portion with 1 tablespoon soured cream and serve with sautéed potatoes and broccoli florets, if desired.

Cook's Tip
Top each portion with 1 tablespoon soured cream to serve, if desired.

Sweet and Sour Meatballs

MAKES 4 TO 6 SERVINGS

1 POUND LEAN GROUND PORK

4 SHALLOTS, FINELY CHOPPED

½ CUP FINELY CHOPPED
MUSHROOMS

1 CUP FRESH BREADCRUMBS

3 TABLESPOONS SUN-DRIED
TOMATO PASTE

FINELY GRATED ZEST 1 LEMON

2 TEASPOONS DRIED
HERBES DE PROVENCE

SALT AND GROUND BLACK PEPPER

2 TABLESPOONS ALL-PURPOSE FLOUR

2 TABLESPOONS OLIVE OIL

1 TABLESPOON CORNSTARCH

¼ CUP RED WINE

1¼ CUPS PASSATA

⅔ CUP UNSWEETENED APPLE JUICE

2 TABLESPOONS RED WINE VINEGAR

2 TABLESPOONS LIGHT SOFT
BROWN SUGAR

◆ Place pork, shallots, mushrooms, breadcrumbs, 2 tablespoons tomato paste, lemon zest, dried herbs, and seasoning in a bowl and mix well.

◆ Divide mixture into 28 equal portions and roll each into a small ball. Roll meatballs in flour, place on a plate, and chill in the refrigerator 20 minutes.

◆ Preheat the slow cooker on HIGH. Heat oil in a skillet, add meatballs, and fry about 10 minutes, or until lightly browned all over, turning occasionally.

◆ Meanwhile, blend cornstarch with red wine in a pan. Stir in passata, apple juice, vinegar, sugar, and remaining 1 tablespoon tomato paste. Heat gently, stirring continuously, until mixture comes to a boil and thickens. Simmer gently 3 minutes.

◆ Transfer meatballs to the cooking pot using a slotted spoon and pour sauce over the top. Cover, reduce temperature to LOW, and cook 6 to 8 hours or until meatballs are cooked and tender.

◆ Serve with egg noodles or rice and stir-fried vegetables, if desired.

Variations
Use tomato juice in place of passata. Use pineapple or orange juice in place of apple juice.

Spicy Sausage and Mushroom Hotpot

MAKES 4 TO 6 SERVINGS

8 THICK SPICY PREMIUM
PORK SAUSAGES

2 TABLESPOONS SUNFLOWER OIL

1 RED ONION, THINLY SLICED

1 GARLIC CLOVE, CRUSHED

1 FRESH RED CHILE,
SEEDED AND FINELY CHOPPED

2 PARSNIPS, DICED

2 CARROTS, THINLY SLICED

2 STALKS CELERY, THINLY SLICED

2 CUPS SLICED CHESTNUT
MUSHROOMS

2 TABLESPOONS ALL-PURPOSE FLOUR

1 CUP VEGETABLE STOCK

1 CUP PASSATA OR TOMATO JUICE

2 TEASPOONS CHILI SAUCE

SALT AND GROUND BLACK PEPPER

4 OR 5 MEDIUM POTATOES,
PEELED AND THINLY SLICED

1 TABLESPOON BUTTER,
MELTED

◆ Preheat the slow cooker on HIGH while preparing ingredients. Broil sausages until lightly browned all over. Cut each sausage into 3 pieces and set aside.

◆ Meanwhile, heat oil in a pan, add onion, garlic, chile, parsnips, carrots, celery, and mushrooms and sauté 5 minutes.

◆ Stir in flour and cook 1 minute, stirring. Gradually add stock and passata or tomato juice, then add chili sauce and seasoning. Bring to a boil, stirring.

◆ Put one third of the vegetable mixture in the cooking pot, then arrange one third of the potato slices over the top. Place half the sausages on top of potatoes. Continue layering vegetables, potatoes, and sausages, finishing with a layer of potatoes.

◆ Cover the cooking pot, reduce the temperature to LOW, and cook 8 to 10 hours, or until cooked.

◆ Brush top layer of potatoes with melted butter and place under a preheated broiler until golden.

Hungarian Goulash

3 TABLESPOONS VEGETABLE OIL

2 LARGE ONIONS, THINLY SLICED

2 GARLIC CLOVES, THINLY SLICED

1 LARGE GREEN BELL PEPPER,
SEEDED AND THINLY SLICED

2 TABLESPOONS ALL-PURPOSE FLOUR

1½ TABLESPOONS PAPRIKA

2 POUNDS BONELESS PORK
SHOULDER, CUT INTO SMALL DICE

1¼ CUPS RED WINE

14-OUNCE CAN CHOPPED TOMATOES

2½ CUPS SLICED BUTTON
MUSHROOMS

1 TEASPOON DRIED THYME

2 BAY LEAVES

◆ Preheat the slow cooker on HIGH while preparing ingredients. Heat 2 tablespoons of the oil in a large pan and sauté onions, garlic, and green bell pepper 5 minutes. Transfer to the cooking pot. Set aside.

◆ Mix flour and paprika together and coat pork with this mixture. Add remaining oil to the pan, then cook pork quickly 5 minutes to brown all over.

◆ Add wine, tomatoes, mushrooms, thyme, bay leaves, and salt and pepper and bring to a boil, stirring. Transfer to the cooking pot and stir to mix.

◆ Cover, reduce temperature to LOW, and cook 8 to 10 hours, or until pork is cooked and tender

◆ Serve goulash with cooked noodles or rice, or with fresh crusty bread, if desired.

Stifado

⅓ CUP VEGETABLE OIL

6 ONIONS, CHOPPED

4 GARLIC CLOVES, CHOPPED

2 POUNDS LEAN STEWING BEEF,
CUT INTO SMALL DICE

2 TABLESPOONS ALL-PURPOSE FLOUR

8 PLUM TOMATOES, PEELED
AND CHOPPED

3 TABLESPOONS TOMATO PASTE

1½ CUPS RED WINE

◆ Preheat the slow cooker on HIGH while preparing ingredients. Heat 3 tablespoons of the oil in a large pan. Add onions and garlic and sauté 5 minutes. Transfer to the cooking pot.

◆ Heat remaining oil in the pan, add beef, and cook until sealed all over. Stir in flour and cook 1 minute, stirring. Add tomatoes, tomato paste, wine, and seasoning and bring to a boil, stirring.

◆ Transfer to the cooking pot and stir to mix. Cover, reduce temperature to LOW, and cook 8 to 10 hours, or until beef is cooked and tender.

◆ Serve with fresh crusty bread, if desired.

Fragrant Ham

MAKES 6 TO 8 SERVINGS

2¹/₂- TO 3-POUND HAM JOINT

*2 MEDIUM PARSNIPS,
QUARTERED LENGTHWISE*

*5 MEDIUM CARROTS,
CUT INTO SMALL CHUNKS*

*1 POUND RUTABAGA,
CUT INTO SMALL CHUNKS*

*2 STALKS CELERY,
CUT INTO SMALL CHUNKS*

*2 CUPS MEDIUM OR DRY CIDER
OR VEGETABLE STOCK*

1 TABLESPOON BROWN SUGAR

1 TABLESPOON RED WINE VINEGAR

1 TABLESPOON BLACK PEPPERCORNS

6 CLOVES

OREGANO SPRIGS, TO GARNISH

◆ Put ham in a large pan, cover with cold water, and let soak 1 to 2 hours.

◆ Preheat the slow cooker on HIGH. Drain ham, return to the pan, and cover with fresh water. Bring to a boil, then rinse, drain, and place in the cooking pot.

◆ Add parsnips, carrots, rutabaga, celery, cider or stock, sugar, vinegar, peppercorns, and cloves to the cooking pot. Cover and cook on HIGH 4 to 6 hours, or until ham and vegetables are cooked and tender.

◆ Lift out ham, slice, and arrange on warmed serving plates. Remove vegetables with a slotted spoon and arrange around ham. Garnish with oregano sprigs and serve.

Lamb and Apricot Tagine

2 TABLESPOONS OLIVE OIL

1½ POUNDS LEAN BONELESS LEG OR SHOULDER OF LAMB, CUT INTO SMALL CUBES

1 LARGE ONION, THINLY SLICED

2 GARLIC CLOVES, CRUSHED

4 CARROTS, THINLY SLICED

1 TABLESPOON ALL-PURPOSE FLOUR

1 TEASPOON TURMERIC

1 TEASPOON GROUND CORIANDER

1 TEASPOON GROUND CUMIN

1 TEASPOON GROUND CINNAMON

SALT AND GROUND BLACK PEPPER

2 CUPS LAMB OR VEGETABLE STOCK

8 OUNCES BUTTON MUSHROOMS

GRATED ZEST 1 LEMON

1 CUP READY-TO-EAT DRIED APRICOTS, CHOPPED

2 TABLESPOONS CLEAR HONEY

CHOPPED FRESH CILANTRO, TO SERVE (OPTIONAL)

◆ Preheat the slow cooker on HIGH while preparing ingredients. Heat oil in a pan, add lamb, and cook in batches until sealed all over. Transfer to the cooking pot using a slotted spoon and set aside.

◆ Add onion, garlic, and carrots to the pan and sauté 5 minutes. Stir in flour, turmeric, coriander, cumin, cinnamon, salt, and pepper. Cook 1 minute, stirring.

◆ Gradually add stock, then add mushrooms and lemon zest and bring to a boil, stirring. Transfer to the cooking pot and stir to mix. Cover, reduce the temperature to LOW, and cook 6 to 8 hours.

◆ Stir in apricots and honey, cover, and cook on LOW an additional 1 to 2 hours, or until lamb is cooked and tender.

◆ Sprinkle with chopped fresh cilantro and serve with couscous, if desired.

Lamb and Bell Pepper Hotpot

MAKES 4 SERVINGS

2 TABLESPOONS SUNFLOWER OIL

8 LEAN LOIN LAMB CHOPS

2 ONIONS, THINLY SLICED

2 RED BELL PEPPERS, SEEDED AND SLICED

3 STALKS CELERY, THINLY SLICED

4 CARROTS, THINLY SLICED

3 BAKING POTATOES, PEELED AND THINLY SLICED

1½ CUPS LAMB OR VEGETABLE STOCK

2 TABLESPOONS TOMATO PASTE

2 TEASPOONS DRIED MIXED HERBS

SALT AND GROUND BLACK PEPPER

1 TABLESPOON BUTTER, MELTED

FRESH HERB SPRIGS, TO GARNISH (OPTIONAL)

◆ Preheat the slow cooker on HIGH while preparing ingredients. Heat oil in a pan, add lamb chops, and cook in batches until sealed all over. Transfer to a plate and set aside.

◆ Add onions, bell peppers, celery, and carrots to the pan and sauté 5 minutes.

◆ Place 4 lamb chops in the bottom of the cooking pot. Arrange one third of potato slices over lamb and top potatoes with half the vegetable mixture. Repeat these layers and finish with a layer of potato slices.

◆ Mix stock, tomato paste, mixed herbs, salt ,and pepper and pour into the cooking pot over lamb and vegetables.

◆ Cover, reduce temperature to LOW, and cook 8 to 10 hours, or until lamb and vegetables are cooked and tender.

◆ Brush top layer of potatoes with melted butter and place under a preheated broiler until golden.

◆ Garnish with fresh herb sprigs to serve, if desired.

Note
This recipe is best cooked in a slow cooker with a minimum capacity of 4½ to 5 quarts.

Vegetarian Dishes

Vegetable Biryani

3 TABLESPOONS SUNFLOWER OIL

3 CARROTS, FINELY CHOPPED

1 MEDIUM POTATO, PEELED AND CUT INTO SMALL CUBES

3 MEDIUM ONIONS, THINLY SLICED

1-INCH PIECE FRESH GINGER, PEELED AND GRATED

2 GARLIC CLOVES, CRUSHED

1 TABLESPOON HOT CURRY PASTE

1 TEASPOON TURMERIC

1/2 TEASPOON GROUND CINNAMON

1 1/4 CUPS AMERICAN EASY-COOK LONG-GRAIN RICE

3 1/4 CUPS VEGETABLE STOCK

SALT AND GROUND BLACK PEPPER

3/4 CUP SMALL CAULIFLOWER FLORETS

3/4 CUP FRESH SHELLED PEAS

1/2 CUP TOASTED CASHEWS

2 TABLESPOONS CHOPPED FRESH CILANTRO

◆ Preheat the slow cooker on HIGH, while preparing ingredients. Heat 2 tablespoons oil in a pan and add carrots, potato, and half the onions. Stir in ginger and garlic and sauté 10 minutes.

◆ Add curry paste, turmeric, cinnamon, and rice and cook, stirring, 1 minute. Pour in stock and bring to boil. Season with salt and pepper. Transfer to the cooking pot, cover, and cook on HIGH 1 hour.

◆ Meanwhile, cook cauliflower and peas in a pan of boiling water 5 minutes. Drain. Stir cauliflower, peas, and cashews into rice mixture, adding a little extra stock if needed. Cover and cook on HIGH an additional 30 to 60 minutes, or until rice is cooked and tender and liquid has been absorbed.

◆ Meanwhile, heat remaining oil in a pan. Add reserved onions and cook, stirring occasionally, 10 to 15 minutes, until crisp and golden. Remove with a slotted spoon, drain on kitchen paper, and set aside.

◆ Stir cilantro into biryani and sprinkle over reserved crisp onions to serve.

Stuffed Bell Peppers

MAKES 4 SERVINGS

*4 LARGE BELL PEPPERS
(ASSORTED COLORS)*

2 TABLESPOONS OLIVE OIL

4 SHALLOTS, FINELY CHOPPED

1 GARLIC CLOVE, CRUSHED

*1/2 CUP FINELY CHOPPED
MUSHROOMS*

1 ZUCCHINI, FINELY CHOPPED

3 CUPS COOKED BROWN RICE

*2 TOMATOES, SKINNED,
SEEDED AND FINELY CHOPPED*

*1/2 CUP PINE NUTS,
FINELY CHOPPED*

*1/2 CUP PITTED BLACK OLIVES,
FINELY CHOPPED*

*2 TABLESPOONS CHOPPED
FRESH MIXED HERBS*

SALT AND GROUND BLACK PEPPER

2/3 CUP VEGETABLE STOCK

◆ Preheat the slow cooker on HIGH while preparing ingredients. Slice tops off bell peppers and remove and discard cores and seeds. Cook peppers and lids in a pan of boiling water 5 minutes. Drain and set aside.

◆ Heat oil in a pan, add shallots, garlic, mushrooms, and zucchini and sauté 5 minutes.

◆ Remove pan from the heat and add rice, tomatoes, pine nuts, olives, herbs, salt, and pepper. Stir well to combine.

◆ Spoon some rice stuffing into each bell pepper and top with lids. Place peppers in the cooking pot. Heat stock in a pan until boiling, then pour it around peppers.

◆ Cover and cook on HIGH 2 to 4 hours, or until peppers are tender.

◆ Serve with fresh crusty bread and a mixed baby leaf salad, if desired.

Potato and Bean Casserole with Tomatoes

1¼ CUPS KIDNEY BEANS, SOAKED
OVERNIGHT AND DRAINED

2 TABLESPOONS OLIVE OIL

1 POUND BABY NEW POTATOES,
HALVED, OR POTATOES,
CUT INTO SMALL CHUNKS

1 LARGE ONION, CHOPPED

2 LEEKS, SLICED

2 GARLIC CLOVES, CHOPPED

1 TEASPOON CUMIN SEEDS

1 TEASPOON PAPRIKA

8-OUNCE CAN CHOPPED TOMATOES

2 TABLESPOONS TOMATO PASTE

1½ CUPS VEGETABLE STOCK

2 TABLESPOONS CHOPPED
FRESH CILANTRO

SALT AND GROUND BLACK PEPPER

PLAIN YOGURT, TO SERVE

◆ Preheat the slow cooker on HIGH. Boil beans in a pan with sufficient water to cover 10 minutes. Rinse and drain beans and set aside.

◆ Meanwhile, heat oil in a large pan, add potatoes, onion, and leeks and sauté 5 minutes.

◆ Stir in garlic, cumin, and paprika and sauté 1 minute. Add tomatoes, tomato paste, stock, and beans. Bring to a boil.

◆ Transfer to the cooking pot, cover, and reduce temperature to LOW. Cook 8 to 12 hours, or until beans are cooked and tender.

◆ Stir in cilantro and salt and pepper to taste. Serve with yogurt and a mixed green salad, if desired.

Root Vegetable Curry

2 TABLESPOONS OLIVE OIL

1 RED ONION, CHOPPED

2 GARLIC CLOVES, CRUSHED

1 FRESH RED CHILE,
SEEDED AND FINELY CHOPPED

1-INCH PIECE FRESH GINGER,
PEELED AND FINELY CHOPPED

1½ POUNDS PREPARED MIXED ROOT
VEGETABLES, SUCH AS SWEET
POTATO, POTATO, CARROTS,
CELERIAC AND RUTABAGA,
CUT INTO SMALL DICE

2 TABLESPOONS ALL-PURPOSE FLOUR

2 TEASPOONS GROUND TURMERIC

2 TEASPOONS GROUND CORIANDER

2 TEASPOONS GROUND CUMIN

1½ CUPS VEGETABLE STOCK

⅔ CUP PASSATA

⅔ CUP GOLDEN RAISINS

SALT AND GROUND BLACK PEPPER

2 OR 3 TABLESPOONS CHOPPED
FRESH CILANTRO

◆ Preheat slow cooker on HIGH while preparing ingredients. Heat oil in a large pan and sauté onion, garlic, chile, and ginger 3 minutes.

◆ Add prepared root vegetables and sauté gently 10 minutes.

◆ Stir in flour, turmeric, coriander, and cumin and cook 1 minute, stirring. Gradually stir in stock and passata, then add golden raisins and salt and pepper.

◆ Bring to a boil, stirring, then transfer to the cooking pot. Cover, reduce the temperature to LOW, and cook 8 to 10 hours, or until vegetables are cooked and tender.

◆ Stir in chopped cilantro. Serve with plain boiled rice, if desired.

Macaroni and Broccoli Bake

MAKES 6 SERVINGS

2 CUPS DRIED MACARONI

1 CUP SMALL BROCCOLI FLORETS

¾ STICK BUTTER

2 LEEKS, THINLY SLICED

½ CUP ALL-PURPOSE FLOUR

3¾ CUPS MILK

1½ CUP SHREDDED CHEDDAR CHEESE

1 TEASPOON PREPARED ENGLISH MUSTARD

12-OUNCE CAN CORN KERNELS, DRAINED

SALT AND GROUND BLACK PEPPER

½ CUP FRESH BREADCRUMBS

⅓ CUP FINELY GRATED FRESH PARMESAN CHEESE

2 TABLESPOONS CHOPPED FRESH CHIVES

◆ Preheat the slow cooker on HIGH while preparing ingredients. Cook macaroni in a pan of boiling water 8 minutes, or until just tender. Add broccoli to the pan the last 3 minutes of cooking time. Drain well and set aside.

◆ Meanwhile, melt 2 tablespoons butter in a pan, add leeks, and sauté 8 to 10 minutes, or until softened. Place on a plate and set aside.

◆ Add remaining butter to the pan with flour and milk and heat gently, whisking continuously, until sauce comes to a boil and thickens. Simmer gently 3 minutes, stirring.

◆ Remove pan from the heat and stir in cheese until it has melted. Add macaroni, broccoli, leeks, mustard, corn, and seasoning and mix well.

◆ Grease the cooking pot. Transfer macaroni mixture to the cooking pot. Cover, reduce the temperature to LOW, and cook 3 to 4 hours.

◆ Preheat the broiler to high. Combine breadcrumbs, Parmesan, and chopped chives and sprinkle evenly over macaroni bake. Broil until golden.

◆ Serve with broiled tomatoes, if desired.

Spicy Root Vegetable Casserole

MAKES 4 TO 6 SERVINGS

2 TABLESPOONS OLIVE OIL

1 ONION, THINLY SLICED

1 GARLIC CLOVE, CRUSHED

3 STALKS CELERY, THINLY SLICED

2 CARROTS, THINLY SLICED

8 OUNCES PEELED RUTABAGA, CUT INTO SMALL DICE

2 SMALL PEELED PARSNIPS, CUT INTO SMALL DICE

2 MEDIUM PEELED POTATOES, CUT INTO SMALL DICE

2 TEASPOONS GROUND CORIANDER

2 TEASPOONS GROUND CUMIN

2 TEASPOONS HOT CHILI POWDER

1 CUP PUY OR GREEN LENTILS, RINSED AND DRAINED

14-OUNCE CAN CHOPPED TOMATOES

3 CUPS VEGETABLE STOCK

SALT AND GROUND BLACK PEPPER

2 TABLESPOONS CHOPPED FRESH CILANTRO

Variation
Use sweet potatoes in place of standard potatoes.

◆ Preheat the slow cooker on HIGH while preparing ingredients. Heat oil in a large pan, add onion, garlic, and celery and sauté 3 minutes.

◆ Add carrots, rutabaga, parsnips, and potatoes and sauté 5 minutes.

◆ Add coriander, cumin, and chili powder and cook 1 minute, stirring. Add lentils, tomatoes, stock, and seasoning and stir to mix. Bring to a boil, stirring, then transfer to the cooking pot.

◆ Cover and cook on HIGH 3 to 4 hours or until vegetables and lentils are cooked and tender.

◆ Stir in cilantro and serve with fresh crusty bread, if desired.

Oriental-style Ratatouille

¼ CUP OLIVE OIL

1 SMALL ONION, FINELY CHOPPED

2 GARLIC CLOVES, FINELY CHOPPED

*4 OR 5 RIPE PLUM TOMATOES,
PEELED AND CHOPPED*

*2 TABLESPOONS TAMARI
(JAPANESE SOY SAUCE)*

*1½ TABLESPOONS RICE WINE
OR DRY SHERRY*

2 TABLESPOONS VEGETABLE STOCK

1 TEASPOON SUGAR

SALT AND GROUND BLACK PEPPER

*1 FRESH GREEN CHILE,
SEEDED AND FINELY CHOPPED*

*2 TEASPOONS CORIANDER SEEDS,
TOASTED AND CRUSHED*

1 SMALL EGGPLANT, DICED

1 CUP SLICED SHIITAKE MUSHROOMS

*2 SMALL ZUCCHINI,
CUT INTO DIAGONAL SLICES*

*1 YELLOW AND 1 RED BELL PEPPER,
CORED, SEEDED AND THINLY SLICED*

*2 TEASPOONS SESAME SEEDS,
TOASTED*

◆ Preheat the slow cooker on HIGH while preparing ingredients. Heat 2 tablespoons of oil in a saucepan. Gently sauté onion 5 minutes.

◆ Add garlic and fry 30 seconds. Stir in tomatoes, tamari, rice wine or sherry, stock, and sugar. Season with salt and pepper to taste. Simmer over low heat 2 minutes, stirring occasionally. Set aside.

◆ Heat remaining oil in a large pan and sauté chile and coriander seeds 1 or 2 minutes.

◆ Add eggplant, mushrooms, zucchini, and bell peppers to the pan and sauté 5 minutes.

◆ Stir in reserved tomato sauce and bring to a boil. Transfer to the cooking pot.

◆ Cover, reduce temperature to LOW, and cook 4 to 8 hours, or until vegetables are cooked to your liking.

◆ Adjust seasoning to taste and stir in sesame seeds. Serve with warm crusty bread and a mixed dark leaf salad, if desired.

Vegetable Chili Bake

MAKES 4 SERVINGS

2 TABLESPOONS SUNFLOWER OIL

6 SHALLOTS, SLICED

2 GARLIC CLOVES, CRUSHED

3 STALKS CELERY, FINELY CHOPPED

1 GREEN BELL PEPPER,
SEEDED AND DICED

1 LARGE FRESH GREEN CHILE,
SEEDED AND FINELY CHOPPED

3 CARROTS, THINLY SLICED

1 CUP PEELED AND DICED
TURNIP OR RUTABAGA

2 TEASPOONS GROUND CUMIN

1 TEASPOON HOT CHILI POWDER

14-OUNCE CAN CHOPPED TOMATOES

2 TABLESPOONS TOMATO PASTE

1 CUP VEGETABLE STOCK

1 CUP SLICED CHESTNUT
MUSHROOMS

15-OUNCE CAN RED KIDNEY BEANS,
RINSED AND DRAINED

SALT AND GROUND BLACK PEPPER

1 TABLESPOON CORNSTARCH

FRESH HERB SPRIGS, TO GARNISH

◆ Preheat the slow cooker on HIGH while preparing ingredients. Heat oil in a pan, add shallots, garlic, celery, green bell pepper, and chile and sauté 3 minutes.

◆ Add carrots and turnip or rutabaga and sauté 5 minutes. Add ground cumin and chili powder and cook 1 minute, stirring.

◆ Add tomatoes, tomato paste, stock, mushrooms, kidney beans, and seasoning and stir to mix. In a small bowl, blend cornstarch with a little water, then stir it into vegetable mixture.

◆ Bring to a boil, stirring, then transfer to the cooking pot. Cover, reduce the temperature to LOW, and cook 6 to 8 hours, or until vegetables are cooked and tender.

◆ Garnish with fresh herb sprigs and serve with cooked rice, if desired.

Fruit and Nut Pilaf

MAKES 4 SERVINGS

1 TABLESPOON OLIVE OIL

1 ONION, FINELY CHOPPED

2 GARLIC CLOVES, CRUSHED

1 FRESH RED CHILE,
SEEDED AND FINELY CHOPPED

1 RED BELL PEPPER,
SEEDED AND DICED

1½ TEASPOONS GROUND CORIANDER

1½ TEASPOONS GROUND CUMIN

1¼ CUPS AMERICAN EASY-COOK
LONG-GRAIN RICE

⅔ CUP GOLDEN RAISINS

⅔ CUP READY-TO-EAT
DRIED APRICOTS, CHOPPED

3 CUPS VEGETABLE STOCK

3 TABLESPOONS DRY SHERRY

SALT AND GROUND BLACK PEPPER

¾ CUP UNSALTED CASHEWS,
TOASTED

2 TABLESPOONS CHOPPED FRESH
CILANTRO

FRESH CILANTRO SPRIGS,
TO GARNISH (OPTIONAL)

◆ Preheat the slow cooker on HIGH while preparing ingredients. Heat oil in a pan, add onion, garlic, chile, and red bell pepper and sauté 5 minutes.

◆ Add coriander, cumin, and rice and cook 1 minute, stirring. Add golden raisins, apricots, stock, sherry, and seasoning and mix well.

◆ Bring to a boil, stirring, then transfer to the cooking pot. Cover and cook on HIGH 1 to 2 hours, or until rice is cooked and tender and all liquid has been absorbed. Stir once halfway through cooking time and add a little extra hot stock, if needed.

◆ Stir in cashews and chopped cilantro. Garnish with fresh cilantro and serve with a green salad, if desired.

Chickpea and Eggplant Casserole

MAKES 6 SERVINGS

1 TEASPOON CUMIN SEEDS

2 TEASPOONS CORIANDER SEEDS

2 TABLESPOONS SESAME SEEDS

2 TEASPOONS DRIED OREGANO

3 TABLESPOONS SHELLED
ALMONDS, TOASTED

3 TABLESPOONS OLIVE OIL

2 ONIONS, FINELY CHOPPED

1 RED BELL PEPPER, SEEDED
AND DICED

1 EGGPLANT, DICED

2 CUPS CHOPPED GREEN BEANS

2 GARLIC CLOVES, CRUSHED

1/2 TEASPOON HOT CHILI POWDER,
OR TO TASTE

14-OUNCE CAN CHOPPED TOMATOES

15-OUNCE CAN CHICKPEAS, DRAINED

1 CUP VEGETABLE STOCK

SALT

3 TABLESPOONS FINELY CHOPPED
FRESH CILANTRO

YOGURT, TO SERVE

◆ Preheat the slow cooker on HIGH while preparing ingredients. Dry-fry cumin, coriander, and sesame seeds together in a heavy-bottomed pan until the aroma rises. Add oregano and fry a few more seconds.

◆ Put seeds, oregano, and nuts in a blender and grind to a powder.

◆ Heat oil in a large pan. Add onions, bell pepper, eggplant, and green beans and sauté 5 minutes. Add garlic, ground seed mixture, and chili powder and cook 2 minutes, stirring.

◆ Add tomatoes, chickpeas, and stock. Bring to a boil, season with a little salt, then transfer to cooking pot. Cover, reduce temperature to LOW, and cook 7 to 9 hours, or until vegetables are cooked and tender.

◆ Check seasoning, adding more salt or chili powder if necessary. Stir in cilantro and serve with yogurt.

Harvest Vegetable Hotpot

MAKES 4 TO 6 SERVINGS

2 TABLESPOONS SUNFLOWER OIL

6 SHALLOTS, SLICED

2 LEEKS, SLICED

2 STALKS CELERY, FINELY CHOPPED

1 RED BELL PEPPER, SEEDED
AND SLICED

1 POUND PREPARED MIXED ROOT
VEGETABLES, SUCH AS CARROTS,
PARSNIPS AND RUTABAGA OR TURNIP,
CUT INTO SMALL CUBES

1½ CUPS SMALL CAULIFLOWER
FLORETS, HALVED

14-OUNCE CAN CHOPPED TOMATOES

⅔ CUP VEGETABLE STOCK

⅔ CUP DRY WHITE WINE OR CIDER

2 TEASPOONS DRIED
HERBES DE PROVENCE

SALT AND GROUND BLACK PEPPER

2 TABLESPOONS CORNSTARCH

4 MEDIUM POTATOES, PEELED
AND THINLY SLICED

1 TABLESPOON BUTTER, MELTED

FRESH HERB SPRIGS,
TO GARNISH

◆ Preheat the slow cooker on HIGH while preparing ingredients. Heat oil in a large pan and sauté shallots, leeks, and celery 5 minutes.

◆ Add red bell pepper, root vegetables, and cauliflower and sauté an additional 5 minutes. Add tomatoes, stock, wine or cider, dried herbs, and seasoning and mix well.

◆ In a small bowl, blend cornstarch with a little water, then stir into vegetable mixture. Bring to a boil, stirring continuously, until mixture thickens. Simmer gently 2 minutes, stirring.

◆ Spoon one third of the vegetable mixture into the cooking pot, then arrange one third of the potato slices over vegetables. Repeat these layers twice more, finishing with a neat layer of potatoes on top.

◆ Cover, reduce the temperature to LOW, and cook 6 to 8 hours, or until vegetables are cooked and tender.

◆ Brush the top with melted butter and place under a preheated broiler until golden. Garnish with fresh herb sprigs. Serve with green beans, if desired.

Cheesy Zucchini Strata

2 TABLESPOONS BUTTER

1 ONION, FINELY CHOPPED

1 SMALL LEEK, THINLY SLICED

2 ZUCCHINI, SLICED

7-OUNCE CAN CORN KERNELS, DRAINED

SALT AND GROUND BLACK PEPPER

9 MEDIUM SLICES OF BREAD, CRUSTS REMOVED AND SLICES CUT INTO FINGERS

3 EGGS

2½ CUPS MILK

2 TABLESPOONS CHOPPED FRESH CHIVES

2 TABLESPOONS CHOPPED FRESH PARSLEY

1 CUP SHREDDED MATURE CHEDDAR CHEESE

◆ Preheat the slow cooker on HIGH while preparing ingredients. Grease a 1½- to 2-quart ovenproof dish and set aside.

◆ Melt butter in a pan, add onion, leek, and zucchini and sauté 8 to 10 minutes or until softened. Remove pan from the heat and stir in corn and seasoning. Set aside.

◆ Place one third of bread in the base of the prepared dish. Top with half the zucchini mixture. Repeat layers, ending with a layer of bread.

◆ Heat milk in a small pan or in a microwave. Whisk together eggs, hot milk, chopped chives and parsley, and seasoning, then pour into the dish over bread and vegetables.

◆ Sprinkle cheese over the top. Cover loosely with greased aluminum foil. Place in the cooking pot of the slow cooker.

◆ Add sufficient boiling water to the cooking pot to come halfway up the sides of the dish. Cover and cook on HIGH 3 to 4 hours (or on LOW 4 to 6 hours), or until lightly set.

◆ Serve with broccoli and cauliflower florets or a mixed leaf salad, if desired.

Desserts

Chocolate Fondue

12 OUNCES BITTERSWEET CHOCOLATE

3 TABLESPOONS BUTTER

1 CUP THICK CREAM

½ TEASPOON GROUND CINNAMON

3 TABLESPOONS BRANDY OR RUM

FOR DIPPING

SELECTION OF PREPARED FRESH FRUIT (SUCH AS STRAWBERRIES, CHERRIES, KIWI FRUIT AND BANANA)

SPONGE FINGERS OR SWEET WAFER BISCUITS

READY-TO-EAT DRIED FRUITS (SUCH AS APRICOTS AND FIGS)

WHOLE NUTS (SUCH AS WALNUTS OR BRAZIL NUTS)

◆ Break chocolate into squares. Place chocolate squares in the cooking pot of the slow cooker with butter, cream, cinnamon, and brandy or rum. Stir to mix.

◆ Cover and cook on LOW 1 to 2 hours, or until all ingredients have melted together, stirring once.

◆ Stir briskly until well combined and smooth, then serve with fresh and dried fruits, sponge fingers, and nuts for dipping.

Apricot Bread Pudding

MAKES 4 TO 6 SERVINGS

3 TABLESPOONS BUTTER, SOFTENED

6 MEDIUM SLICES OF BREAD, CRUSTS REMOVED

1 CUP READY-TO-EAT DRIED APRICOTS, FINELY CHOPPED

¼ CUP LIGHT SOFT BROWN SUGAR

2 TEASPOONS GROUND MIXED SPICE

3 EGGS

2 CUPS LIGHT CREAM

◆ Preheat the slow cooker on HIGH while preparing ingredients. Lightly grease a 7- to 8-cup ovenproof soufflé or similar dish that will sit in the cooking pot.

◆ Spread butter over bread slices, then cut bread into small triangles or fingers. Arrange half of the bread in the bottom of the prepared dish, butter-side up.

◆ Mix together apricots, sugar, and mixed spice and sprinkle over bread. Top with remaining bread, butter-side up.

◆ Beat eggs and cream together and pour over bread. Set aside 30 minutes to allow bread to absorb some of the liquid.

◆ Cover with greased aluminum foil, then place in the cooking pot. Add sufficient boiling water to come halfway up the sides of the dish. Cover the cooking pot, reduce the temperature to LOW, and cook 3 to 5 hours or until custard has set.

◆ Serve with fresh fruit, such as sliced peaches, nectarines or apricots, if desired.

Variations
Use golden raisins or ready-to-eat dried pears in place of apricots. Use ground cinnamon or ginger in place of mixed spice.

Fresh Lemon Sponge Pudding

MAKES 6 SERVINGS

¼ CUP LIGHT CORN SYRUP

1 STICK BUTTER (SOFTENED) OR MARGARINE

⅔ CUP LIGHT SOFT BROWN SUGAR

2 EGGS

FINELY GRATED ZEST 1 LEMON

1½ CUPS SELF-RISING FLOUR, SIFTED

2 OR 3 TABLESPOONS MILK

◆ Preheat the slow cooker on HIGH while preparing ingredients. Lightly grease a 4-cup pudding basin and line the bottom with a small circle of non-stick baking parchment. Spoon syrup into the bottom of the prepared basin and set aside.

◆ In a bowl, beat butter or margarine and sugar together until pale and creamy. Gradually beat in eggs, then beat in lemon zest. Fold in flour and add enough milk to make a soft, dropping consistency.

◆ Spoon mixture into the basin over syrup and level the surface. Cover loosely with a double layer of greased aluminum foil and place in the cooking pot of the slow cooker.

◆ Add sufficient boiling water to the cooking pot to come halfway up the sides of the basin. Cover and cook on HIGH 3 to 4 hours, or until sponge is cooked and a skewer inserted in the center comes out clean.

◆ Carefully turn out onto a warmed serving plate. Serve with custard, cream, or ice cream, if desired.

Plum Pudding

MAKES 8 TO 10 SERVINGS

1 CUP RAISINS

1 CUP GOLDEN RAISINS

⅓ CUP DRIED CRANBERRIES

⅓ CUP READY-TO-EAT DRIED APRICOTS, FINELY CHOPPED

2 TABLESPOONS BRANDY OR SHERRY

FINELY GRATED ZEST AND JUICE 1 SMALL ORANGE

FINELY GRATED ZEST AND JUICE 1 LEMON

½ CUP ALL-PURPOSE FLOUR

2 TEASPOONS GROUND MIXED SPICE

2 CUPS FRESH BREADCRUMBS

1 CUP SHREDDED BEEF OR VEGETABLE SUET

⅔ CUP LIGHT SOFT BROWN SUGAR

3 EGGS, BEATEN

◆ Put raisins, golden raisins, and dried cranberries and apricots in a bowl, add brandy or sherry and orange and lemon zest and stir to mix well. Cover and let soak several hours or overnight.

◆ Preheat the slow cooker on HIGH while preparing pudding. Lightly grease a 6- to 6½-cup pudding basin and line the bottom with a small circle of non-stick baking parchment.

◆ Mix flour, mixed spice, breadcrumbs, suet, and sugar in a bowl. Add dried fruits and soaking liquid and eggs and beat together until mixed. Spoon mixture into the prepared basin and level the surface.

◆ Cover with a sheet of non-stick baking parchment and cover this with a double layer of pleated aluminum foil. Secure with string. Place in the cooking pot of the slow cooker.

◆ Add sufficient boiling water to the cooking pot to come three-quarters of the way up the sides of the basin. Cover and cook on HIGH 8 to 12 hours, or until pudding is cooked, topping up with boiling water as necessary.

◆ Turn pudding out onto a warmed serving plate and serve immediately. Alternatively, allow to cool, then re-cover and store in a cool, dry place until required.

Chocolate Sponge Cake

1½ STICKS BUTTER, SOFTENED

1 CUP LIGHT SOFT BROWN SUGAR

3 EGGS, BEATEN

1½ CUPS SELF-RISING FLOUR

¼ CUP COCOA POWDER

FEW DROPS VANILLA EXTRACT

1 OR 2 TABLESPOONS MILK

⅔ CUP THICK CREAM
(OPTIONAL)

CONFECTIONERS' SUGAR,
FOR SIFTING (OPTIONAL)

◆ Preheat the slow cooker on HIGH. Lightly grease and line a 7-inch round deep cake tin. Cream butter and sugar together in a bowl until lightly fluffy, then gradually beat in eggs. Sift in flour and cocoa powder and fold in lightly with vanilla extract. Add enough milk to make a soft dropping consistency.

◆ Spoon into tin and level surface. Cover loosely with greased aluminum foil. Stand the tin on top of a plain metal pastry cutter in cooking pot of slow cooker. Add sufficient boiling water to come halfway up sides of tin. Cover and cook on HIGH 2 to 3 hours, or until a skewer inserted in center of cake comes out clean.

◆ Lift tin out of the slow cooker and let stand 5 minutes. Turn cake out of the tin and let cool completely on a wire rack. Fill with whipped thick cream and sift over confectioners' sugar to serve, if desired.

Moist Cider Cake

1⅔ CUPS MIXED DRIED FRUIT

2 TABLESPOONS MIXED PEEL

1 CUP MEDIUM CIDER

1 STICK BUTTER, DICED

1 CUP LIGHT SOFT BROWN SUGAR

½ CUP SIEVED COOKED POTATOES

2 CUPS ALL-PURPOSE FLOUR

2 TEASPOONS GROUND MIXED SPICE

1 TEASPOON BICARBONATE OF SODA

1 EGG, BEATEN

◆ Soak dried fruit and mixed peel in cider in a non-metallic bowl overnight. Preheat the slow cooker on HIGH. Lightly grease and line a 7-inch round deep cake tin.

◆ Transfer soaked fruit mixture to a saucepan and add butter and sugar. Bring to boil slowly, stirring occasionally. Simmer 10 minutes.

◆ Remove from heat, let cool slightly, then mix in potatoes, flour, mixed spice, bicarbonate of soda, and beaten egg to give a very soft dropping consistency. Pour mixture into tin and level surface. Cover loosely with greased aluminum foil.

◆ Stand tin on top of a metal pastry cutter in cooking pot. Add boiling water to come halfway up sides of tin. Cover and cook on HIGH 5 to 7 hours, or until a skewer inserted in center of cake comes out clean.

◆ Lift tin out of slow cooker and let stand 5 minutes. Turn cake out of tin and let cool completely on a wire rack.

Tipsy Pears

MAKES 4 SERVINGS

4 LARGE PEARS

2 CUPS RED WINE

⅔ CUP UNSWEETENED APPLE JUICE

½ CUP LIGHT SOFT BROWN SUGAR

2 CINNAMON STICKS

4 WHOLE CLOVES

FRESH MINT SPRIGS, TO DECORATE

◆ Preheat the slow cooker on HIGH while preparing ingredients. Carefully peel pears, then cut them in half and remove and discard cores. Place in the cooking pot and set aside.

◆ Place red wine, apple juice, and sugar in a saucepan and heat gently, stirring, until sugar has dissolved. Add cinnamon sticks and cloves, then bring to a boil.

◆ Pour over pears in the cooking pot. Cover, reduce the temperature to LOW, and cook 6 to 8 hours or until pears are tender.

◆ Carefully remove pears from liquid and keep hot. Remove and discard cinnamon sticks and cloves.

◆ Pour liquid into a pan and boil rapidly until it is reduced and thickened slightly. Spoon liquid over pears and decorate with fresh mint sprigs. Serve warm or cold with thick soured cream or yogurt, if desired.

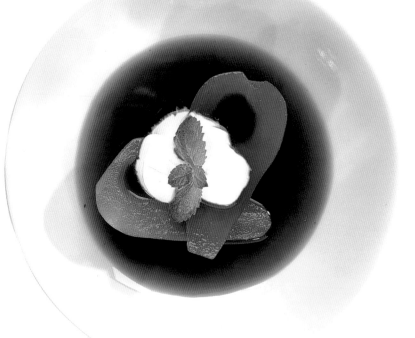

Rice Pudding with Orange

MAKES 4 TO 6 SERVINGS

2 TABLESPOONS BUTTER

½ CUP PUDDING RICE,
RINSED AND DRAINED

½ CUP GRANULATED SUGAR

3 CUPS MILK

1 CUP EVAPORATED MILK

FINELY GRATED ZEST 1 LARGE ORANGE

SEEDS FROM 3 CARDAMOM PODS,
CRUSHED

PARED ORANGE RIND, TO DECORATE

◆ Grease the inside of the cooking pot of the slow cooker with a little butter.

◆ Place rice, sugar, milk, evaporated milk, orange zest, and crushed cardamom seeds in the cooking pot and stir to mix. Dot with any remaining butter.

◆ Cover and cook on HIGH 3 to 4 hours (or on LOW 4 to 6 hours), or until the rice is cooked and most of the liquid has been absorbed. Stir once or twice during the final 2 hours of cooking, if possible.

◆ Decorate with pared orange rind. Serve with stewed fresh fruit, such as plums, or warm fruit compote, if desired.

Crème Caramel

1 CUP GRANULATED SUGAR

4 EGGS

½ TEASPOON VANILLA EXTRACT

2½ CUPS MILK

◆ Preheat the slow cooker on HIGH while preparing crème caramel. Grease a 7-inch soufflé dish or similar ovenproof dish. Set aside.

◆ Put ⅔ cup sugar in a small pan with ⅔ cup water. Heat gently, stirring, until sugar has dissolved, then bring to a boil and boil without stirring, until mixture caramelizes to a golden brown. Pour into the prepared dish and set aside.

◆ Put eggs, vanilla extract, and remaining sugar in a bowl and whisk together lightly. Set aside.

◆ Warm milk in a saucepan, then pour onto egg mixture, whisking continuously. Strain over cooled caramel. Cover the dish with aluminum foil, then place in the cooking pot of the slow cooker.

◆ Add sufficient boiling water to the cooking pot to come halfway up the sides of the dish. Cover, reduce temperature to LOW, and cook 5 to 6 hours or until set (a knife inserted in the center should come out clean when it is cooked).

◆ Remove the dish from the slow cooker, uncover, and let cool, then chill several hours.

◆ Gently ease dessert away from the sides of the dish and carefully turn out onto a serving plate. Serve with fresh fruit, such as raspberries, if desired.

Winter Fruit Compote

MAKES 6 SERVINGS

½ CUP DRIED APPLE RINGS

1 CUP READY-TO-EAT
DRIED APRICOTS

¾ CUP READY-TO-EAT
DRIED PRUNES

⅓ CUP GOLDEN RAISINS

⅓ CUP RAISINS

1 PEAR, PEELED, CORED
AND CUT INTO 8

2 CINNAMON STICKS

THINLY PARED RIND 1 LEMON

2½ CUPS UNSWEETENED
APPLE JUICE

FRESH MINT SPRIGS, TO DECORATE

◆ Preheat the slow cooker on HIGH 15 to 20 minutes. Put apple rings, dried apricots, prunes, golden raisins, raisins, and pear in cooking pot. Gently stir in cinnamon sticks, lemon rind, and apple juice.

◆ Cover, reduce the temperature to LOW, and cook 8 to 10 hours, or until fruit is plumped up and tender.

◆ Remove and discard cinnamon sticks and lemon rind. Decorate with mint sprigs.

◆ Serve compote warm or cold, with thick soured cream, mascarpone cheese or plain yogurt, if desired.

Variations
Use your own choice of mixed dried fruits in similar proportions to above, if preferred.

Index